RAPID TRANSIT
IN AND ABOUT
NEW YORK CITY

Transportation
Library

HE
4491
.N57
1925

The Municipal Art Society

of

New York.

COMMITTEE ON CITY PLAN:

CALVIN TOMKINS, Chairman

JOHN DE WITT WARNER,
FREDERICK S. LAMB,
MILO ROY MALTBIE.

J. G. PHELPS STOKES,
CHARLES R. LAMB,
HENRY W. SACKETT.

A Discussion of the Rapid Transit Problem in and about New York City by the City Plan Committee of the Municipal Art Society.

SEPTEMBER 1, 1905.

The within collection of reports were published in the Bulletins of the Municipal Art Society issued between November and May, 1904 and 1905. They constitute a discussion of varying phases of the transit problem in New York City. Since an adequate solution of this matter at this time is of the last importance, it has been thought well to bind together and reissue the separate reports as a contribution to the general discussion which is now about to take place.

The Bulletins may be briefly characterized as follows:

Bulletin No. 14—A general discussion at length, of local rapid transit, with a table of contents annexed.

Bulletin No. 11, by James C. Bayles, discusses pipe galleries in connection with subways.

Bulletins Nos. 16, 17 and 22 relate to subway advertising and incidentally take cognizance of the legal status of the subways, and of the relations which exist between the City and its subway agents.

Bulletins Nos. 18 and 19 (and in a measure No. 22) discuss the franchise grant recently made to the New York and New Jersey Company by the Rapid Transit Commission. This grant differs from that made to the Interborough Company, in that it provides for construction by the concessionaire. The franchise included in the grant is perpetual through Christopher street as far as Sixth avenue, and its further extension eastward through Eighth street and northward through Sixth avenue to Thirty-second street is made for a period of twenty-five years, reserving to the City the option of recovery at the expiration of that period on repayment of the cost to the grantee.

Bulletin No. 20 constitutes a criticism of the routes as proposed at the time of publication, by the Chief Engineer of the Rapid Transit Commission. It also attempts to bring to public attention the great powers entrusted to the Commission together with their attendant responsibilities. The present independent position of the City potentially to control its subway transit is noted and the vital necessity for maintaining such control dwelt upon.

Bulletin No. 24, discusses the report of the Rapid Transit Commission's Committee on Plans and Contracts, dated April 13, 1905, and consists of a brief review of the principles set forth in previous bulletins of the Society, as applied to the important provisions of the above report, many of which provisions have since been formally adopted by the Commission.

As the matter now stands (September, 1905) the principal approaches to lower Manhattan by superficial subways have been examined into by the Rapid Transit Commission and routes along them have been recommended. The Board of Estimate and Apportionment will soon act upon the recommendations of the Commission and the policy of the City regarding its trunk line approaches will be determined for years to come. The question thus arises as to what extent the City shall continue to maintain control over its circulatory system—

1st. As regards service, including transfers.

2d. As regards extensions and rearrangements, which will be made necessary by the City's rapid growth and development.

CALVIN TOMKINS, Chairman,

City Plan Committee, Municipal Art Society.

A Report on Subway Transit by the Executive Committee of the New York Board of Trade and Transportation is here inserted for convenient reference following the Bulletins of the Municipal Art Society.

Municipal Art Society
of
New York.

BULLETIN No. 14.

COMMITTEE ON CITY PLAN:

CALVIN TOMKINS, Chairman.
JOHN DE WITT WARNER,   J. G. PHELPS STOKES,
FREDERICK S. LAMB,   CHARLES R. LAMB,
MILO ROY MALTBIE,   HENRY W. SACKETT.

REPORT

ON

RAPID TRANSIT IN NEW YORK CITY

In 1903 the Municipal Art Society published its first bulletin on "Passenger Transportation" in New York City. A year has now elapsed, during which period the situation has rapidly developed. In this, its revised report, the City Plan Committee again calls attention to the cardinal principles of passenger transportation.

This Society early recognized that settlement of the structural plan of the city should precede suggestions for its embellishment. *The City Problem.*

Commercial needs and social opportunity outweigh all other considerations. Increase of population without consequent increase of congestion constitutes the crucial city problem. Distribution of population over an ever widening area is the best solution; and adequate and cheap transport between home and work the first need to this end.

<small>Decoration should follow Design.</small> From the aesthetic standpoint it may be added that, until the general lines of transit have been determined upon, it is impracticable to plan decorative features. For example, the location of a park, a monument, or a public building, if made without regard to the transportation systems, might be rendered of little effect either by the laying out of new thoroughfares which would cut directly through it and make necessary its removal, or by leaving it stranded without adequate access or perspective. To produce the best results great care must be exercised in the location of public structures; but it is evident that until the street plan and lines of transit have been determined upon it is impossible to decide what points constitute the most advantageous locations.

<small>Criticism and Improvement.</small> Discussion of such matters as park improvements or extensions arouse few or no antagonisms and become largely questions of what the city can afford. Discussion relating to the locating and grouping of public buildings and to street rearrangement is likely to stir the strong opposition only of small groups of property-owners. But discussion of the planning or use of transport facilities at once attracts the attention of the many, who are personally interested as stock-holding concessionaries of the public utilities of the city, and of the general public that uses them; and as a consequence favorable and unfavorable criticism is much more general and spirited. But the beauty and convenience of the city depend to a greater degree upon proper solution of its transit problem than upon any other factor. The following discussion is therefore submitted for consideration and criticism, the more so since it is essential that a sound public opinion be developed without delay.

<small>Causes of Growth of the City.</small> New York reflects the growth of the whole country more than any other city. All important East and West trunk lines tend hither; the steamship business of the port is rapidly increasing; the proposed enlargement of the Erie Canal, and the deepening

of the channel from the Upper Bay to Sandy Hook are equally signs and factors of our city growth. The terminal changes projected—by the Pennsylvania Railroad at Cortlandt street and at Ninth avenue and Thirty-second street; by the Delaware, Lackawanna and Western Railroad; by the New York Central Railroad at the Grand Central Station; by New Jersey roads, through a tunnel to a great terminal station at Christopher street, and the connection to be made between the Pennsylvania and the New York, New Haven and Hartford R. R.'s through Brooklyn—all indicate how urgent is some comprehensive plan for intra-mural transport commensurate with the transportation systems of the country and world converging at our gates.

Assumed that the question of transport must have precedence in any plan of city development, present needs for sudden expansion make this a most critical period of our growth. Mistakes now made will be difficult to correct, involving, as they must, our main arteries of travel.* _{Critical Period.}

Difficulties and Mistakes.

Lower Manhattan constitutes both the objective and departing point for the daily tides of travel. The strain on facilities incident to the rush hours in the morning and in the evening; the long narrow configuration of the island with its crowded and insufficient transit lines converging at the south; the tidal water belt which surrounds it on the east, west and south; its tall buildings, housing an unprecedented factory, office and tenement population to the acre; its street system planned in many respects for obsolete conditions—all these add difficulties to our transit problem, with which other cities do not have to contend. _{Peculiar Difficulties.}

---

*This report does not discuss betterments in connection with surface travel, which subject has formed the basis of an admirable report published by the Merchants' Association, September, 1903. Their report clearly indicates the difficulties which have resulted from the development by private capital of the city's transit system. In seeking to find remedies for the deplorable conditions which exist, it at the same time affords the most striking illustration of the undesirability of permitting public transit to fall into private hands, without adequate supervision and control by the municipality.—Bulletin No. 5, by the Thoroughfares Committee of the Municipal Art Society, discusses proposed street changes in their relation to transportation and growth.

Localized Manhattan Congestion. It is evident that the greatest degree of congestion is now and will continue to be localized in a part of one borough and that this congestion tends seriously to increase in direct proportion to the growth of the whole city and as transport facilities to and from other boroughs are made more adequate.

Avoid Forestalling. These conditions offer additional reasons why the situation should be promptly and broadly dealt with before the opportunity shall have been forestalled. Up to the present the city officials and the Rapid Transit Commission have from time to time invited or waited for transport companies to suggest such extensions or connections with new subways or elevated lines (Pennsylvania R. R. Co., Interborough R. R. Co., New York City Railway Co. and New York and New Jersey Co., etc.) as, in the judgment of these corporations would best serve their own interests and shut out rivals. This policy is inexcusable, for not merely has the city long needed better transit facilities, but it is so far from being dependent on existing franchise corporations that instead it has them at its mercy.

Private Exploitation. For many years it has been the custom to farm out the privilege of passenger transport within the City of New York to numerous traction companies for long terms and without adequate guarantee for controlling the service. Exploitation of these privileges for dividends and stock-watering profits has resulted in a congested and unsatisfactory service.*

Relations Principal Transport Cos. So far as concerns the public, the great transport interests of New York constitute a single combine of three mutually jealous groups, the controlling interests steadily trending more perfectly to coalesce, *i. e., Interborough,* controlling the Manhattan and Bronx elevated and subway systems, the Brooklyn

*As fast as the street railroad company's or the gas company's, or the electrical company's earnings thus increase, its old stock is converted into bonds and new stock issued to represent that increment. The new stock is sold to the public with fabulous profits for the syndicate managers. Legislative regulations of rates is then resisted on the ground that the unfortunate stockholders would lose their dividends. The State is put into a dilemma in which it ought not to be—a dilemma between doing justice to the public who have made the increment, and doing mercy to the ignorant stockholders who have invested their savings in the new stock. The profit of the promoters is unreachable.—ED. B. WHITNEY, *Yale Review.*

subways and the Queens surface railway lines; the *New York City Railway Co.*, controlling the Manhattan and Bronx surface lines, and the *Brooklyn Rapid Transit*, controlling the elevated and surface lines of Brooklyn.* In addition there is to be considered the local influence of the New York Central Railroad, which company is engaged in great terminal improvements and is preparing to install electric traction south of Croton; and the local influence the Pennsylvania Railway Company will exercise through the agency of its tunnel, its Brooklyn and Bronx Belt-line, and the community of ownership which exists between it and New Jersey and Long Island steam and trolley lines.

In extending its own system of underground roads the city may well be served by utilizing through short-term leases the experience acquired by the management of these corporations. But no such steps should be taken as shall place the essential features of the municipally owned system beyond the power of the City to control them. The interests of the transportation corporations should be made subservient to the general public interest instead of allowed to dominate it, as has been the case heretofore. Municipal Independence.

Transit needs have been so neglected till the demand and necessity for them have become so urgent that the public are frequently forced to choose between ulterior good and immediate convenience; and franchises and licenses which would not otherwise be granted are under such conditions given for utterly inadequate consideration. This policy• fits in so well with that of the street railways (which find their greatest profit in highly congested traffic) that it has characterized the relations of public officials to street railway companies in New York City. Indeed, similar reasons were urged by the Rapid Transit Commission at the last session of the legislature as the argument why they should be given power over additional expenditure and over the East River bridges without waiting to have amended the obsolete law which compels the City to enter into needlessly disadvantageous contracts for new subways; their argument being that such enabling legislation should not be associated in the same bill with that which the Com- Delays, Crises, Sacrifices.

---

* Staten Island transit lines not included.

mission was seeking to have passed—since antagonisms would be aroused that would delay the acquisition of additional rapid transit facilities.

That the Rapid Transit Commission originally adhered to correct principles is evident from the following extracts taken from their Report of 1902.

<small>Principles stated by Rapid Transit Commission.</small>

From Page 12:

"Early in 1902 the Board was called upon to defend the essential proposition upon which it had been constituted. This was that the use of the underground and overhead portions of the streets of New York for railroad purposes should proceed according to a harmonious and far-seeing plan, possible only if all such uses, and every such use, of the streets were to be subject to the jurisdiction of the Rapid Transit Board or of some other single like authority which should represent the interests of the entire city, and be so organized as to be able to carry out consistently and efficiently a plan requiring years and perhaps many years for completion."

Extract letter President A. E. Orr to Wm. Barclay Parsons, Chief Engineer, Rapid Transit Commission:

Page 30:

"The enormously valuable property of the city in its streets shall not be improvidently granted or used without a far-sighted regard to the future development and necessities of rapid transit and transportation within its limits. Whether railroad construction and operation be municpal or under control of private corporations, it is now the settled policy of the city that no railroad use of the streets shall needlessly obstruct future rapid transit or other future and profitable use of the streets for transportation purposes. Every future grant of such a street right is to be made with the utmost practicable regard to all other municipal purposes, present and future."

Page No. 67:

"It is therefore clear that the public now has a right to expect from this Board the preparation of a general and far-reaching system of rapid transit, covering the whole City of New York in all its five boroughs. * * *

"The far-reaching plan I have suggested could not, of course, be carried out at once, or, perhaps, completely carried out for many years. But if such a plan be now wisely prepared and the streets of New York be dedicated to tunnel railroad purposes,* with a proper regard to the long and, no doubt, splendid future of the city, two things may reasonably be expected. First, that rapid transit construction will proceed upon the lines laid down as rapidly as the means of the city and the amount of private capital ready for rapid investment will permit. And, second, that relatively unimportant

---

* Not elevated road.

franchises will not be granted in such a way or special routes be so devised as to prevent or obstruct a permanent and sufficient programme.

"It is my conclusion from all this that in laying out the east side line you should study the whole rapid transit situation of all five boroughs and that your report should aid the Board to prepare and submit to the local authorities the comprehensive plan for the entire city which I have suggested, the same to be carried out in sections or instalments, as financial conditions shall from time to time permit."

It would scarcely be inferred that these words of wisdom were those of a commission that up to date still leaves undone the very duty in question, imposed upon it in 1894.

Of the disastrous consequences that we have suffered from disregard by the Rapid Transit Commission of its own good advice, a few examples must suffice, e. g.:

1. We are now told (a) that the Belmont subway is so located opposite the bridge entrance that a direct westerly loop plan for continuous traffic from Brooklyn to the North river connecting with all Manhattan north and south lines, thus accommodating Brooklyn residents and doing away with the crush at the bridge entrance, is impracticable; and (b) that the only practical substitutes are either to deface City Hall Park by elevated railroad structures or to deflect the bridge tracks at a right angle along Centre street. That is: The Commission has permitted the Belmont system to be so built that for seventy-five years to come it can obstruct any plan either of municipal operation or other competing service, of which this bridge (the City's own property) is a factor. As to the Rapid Transit Commission's engineers, their only answer must be the confession that they failed to anticipate the conditions of the near future. (See Plate E.) *Sealing of Brooklyn Bridge Subway Entrance.*

This Society, however, is confident that the future is not so far forestalled as (in excuse for proceeding actually to forestall it) the Commission and its engineers are swift to admit. In short, the good faith and competence of those responsible will be judged by the extent to which they find best remedies at least sacrifice— instead of giving present subway contractors further monopoly, hopelessly disfiguring the city, and dooming Brooklyn residents to perpetual inconvenience. Our Society is advised that by slightly changing (and greatly bettering) the grade of the Bel- *Opening of Same.*

mont subway between Duane street and the loop crossing at the post-office there could be secured plenty of room for a crosstown loop subway under City Hall Park, thus continuing bridge service to the North river.

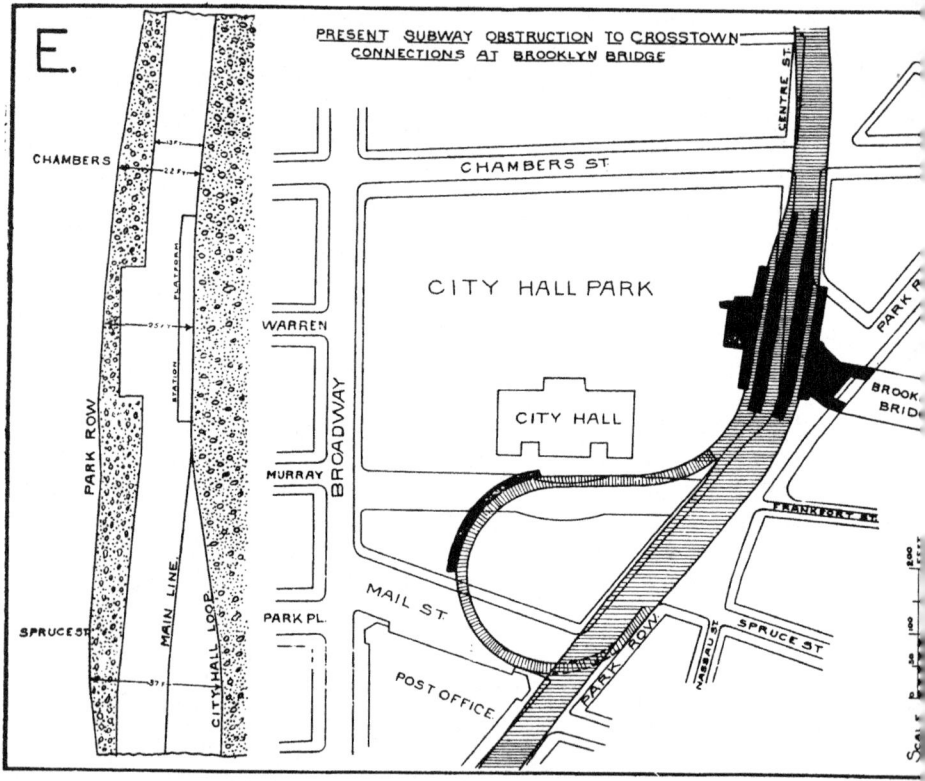

Insufficiency of Lower Broadway and Brooklyn Tunnel.

(2) In providing through lower Broadway and under the East river for the Brooklyn extension of the Manhattan subway such a route was adopted that the larger portion of the present Brooklyn bridge traffic (with any increase from the Manhattan subway) would naturally take it: That is to say, during the "rush hours" 100,000 per hour would wish to be carried in one direction. But as planned, this tunnel extension between the Battery and Brooklyn is a mere "switch" (of one track in each direction) from an originally planned Broadway subway of but one track each way

below Ann street. With trains of six cars seating fifty passengers, each running on 1½-minute headway, the full capacity would be 12,000 per hour; while with eight-car trains and but minute headway (longer trains and shorter headway than can safely be counted on) this would be 24,000 per hour. It can only be guessed how far these figures may be reduced by the switch, etc., conditions. Moreover, it is startling to find that the Commission's engineer has estimated the Brooklyn traffic over this extension at between one-fifth and one-half—say one-third at first—of this single-track capacity.

If this extension is now being built on this plan one can imagine Brooklyn's disappointment when it tries to use it. If it is not so built, the Rapid Transit Commission will have to explain why, after offering such a scheme for competition, the successful bidder was allowed radically to change it.

(3) There has never been a time when any such numbers wanted finally to stop at the bridge entrance or primarily to start therefrom as to have made any crush there. On the contrary, this crush has been occasioned by those who had started (or who would have preferred to start) from some other point, or by those who had no occasion to leave the cars at the present bridge entrance (preferring to be carried on more nearly to where they did want to stop). This inconvenience has been due to the squabbling of private franchise corporations so well united as to head off any solution by municipal operation but mutually so jealous that they could not agree on connections, and so ordered their passengers " all out " at Park row. It must be assumed that the Rapid Transit Commission has known these facts as well as have the rest of us. But if so, then again: Why was not the bridge crush ended years ago? Why does it harbor such a plan as the one lately suggested by which City Hall Park and its environs are to be sacrificed? *Bridge Crush.*

(4) After a generation of slowly mitigated squalor, within two years, at great expense, Fourth avenue, in Brooklyn, has been made a grand boulevard with asphalt driveways, turfed plots and beautiful trees. It is currently stated that this work must now be destroyed for subway construction, or at great expense and inconvenience a street less eligible for this purpose substituted therefor. *Unnecessary Spoliation of Fourth Avenue, Brooklyn.*

Had the principle of the early adoption of a comprehensive plan been followed, the City would not have been put to this expense.

Indeed, as to the Rapid Transit Commission's work as a whole, Mr. Parsons, the Commission's Engineer, admits:

<small>Inadequacy of Manhattan Subway now Built.</small>

"The tremendous increase in passenger travel on all lines clearly indicates that when the tunnel subway system now under construction is completed, it will almost immediately be congested so that no great amount of permanent relief can be counted upon."

Essential Principles of Rapid Transit.

<small>Municipal Control.</small>

FIRST—*Control by the City. Continuous and effective control by the City is the essential condition of any satisfactory solution of the transit problem.*

Such control cannot be secured by mere contract, as experience with existing elevated and surface roads has clearly shown. Actually to control, the City must be able—in the event of unsatisfactory service—to resume all concessions and either release or operate, as it sees fit. This can be accomplished by means of short-term leases, with option to the City of termination at any time on payment of indemnity on specified basis.* The City is already committed to municipal ownership of its franchises, so that the proposed change is one of degree only.

<small>Term of Lease.</small>

Interested as is this Society in city plan, rather than finances or policy, our Committee refrains from discussing this question from other standpoints. But, to leave the City free to adopt and develop proper transport plans, we believe no lease should be made for a longer period than twenty years when the City pays for the line, or for a longer period than ten years when, in addition, the City equips the line.

As stated by Mr. Shepard, of counsel for the Rapid Transit Commission:

<small>Statement Edw. M. Shepard.</small>

"It is said with very great force that no matter how careful you are with your contract provisions when you make a contract for fifty years, nevertheless, if you with-

---

* It is essential that the terms of different franchises should expire at the same time, although they need not be necessarily of the same duration.

hold the right to take the road from the company, the City does not perfectly and presently control operation. Therefore, in my opinion, formed upon the history of New York rapid transit, every effort should be directed to making the term of the lease the shortest possible. When I say the shortest possible term, I mean the shortest term that is consistent with the assumption by private persons or private capital of the financial risk involved to the lessee bound to a rental."

Massachusetts has always insisted upon this policy of revocable grants, and Boston has maintained control over its transit system by means of this law and by retaining ownership and control of the subways in the congested part of the city through which the elevated and surface roads must necessarily pass.

Massachusetts Experience.

"The fundamental mistake has consisted in treating franchise grants as contracts, unalterable without the consent of both parties, like ordinary contracts concerning property. Governments, like individuals, may properly enough enter into contracts relating to property, and such contracts when made should be respected; but governments ought not by contract to divest themselves of governmental functions, as they do to an extent when they surrender partial control of the public streets, by giving to private interests definite-term structural rights therein. * * * The City can control completely only when it is in a position to terminate at any time the right of use claimed by any person or corporation that may choose to defy the will of the City in any respect. In other words, the grant terminable at the will of the governing authorities is the only kind under which the City can be sure of its ability to dominate the situation at all times. * * *" (Geo. C. Sikes, "Atlantic Monthly," March, 1903.)

"One feature in the franchise granted to the Massachusetts companies immediately attracts notice; from the beginning they were, and still almost invariably are, in terms perpetual, while in reality legally revocable at the discretion of local boards. In this respect they are peculiar, almost anomalous; for, as a rule, both in this country and in Europe concessions have been granted private companies for fixed periods of time only, during which the franchise, or concession, is in the nature of a binding contract.

"In theory, such a franchise is to the last degree illogical. It can be compared only to a lease, terminable at will by the lessor, and without provision for the compensation of the lessee. Such a system, if suggested, would naturally be pronounced impracticable, if not absurd, and it would be assumed that private capital would never embark in ventures so lacking in the element of permanence and security. Yet in Massachusetts this has not proved to be the case; nor can it be said that the system has, for the half century it has been in use, worked otherwise than on the whole satisfactory. * * *

"In the course of the protracted hearings before the Committee it was very noticeable that no change was advocated by the representatives of the municipalities or of the companies, nor, apparently, did the suggestion of such a change commend itself to either. Some amendments in detail of the existing law and partial measures of protection against possible orders of sudden, ill-considered or aggressive revocation were suggested; but it was evident that, while the municipalities wanted to retain as a weapon— a sort of discussion bludgeon—the right of revocation at will, the companies preferred, on the whole, a franchise practically permanent though never absolutely certain, to a fixed contract tenure for a shorter term, subject to the danger of alteration at every periodic renewal. There is probably no possible system productive of only good results and in no respects open to criticism; but, in fairness, the Committee found itself forced to conclude that the Massachusetts franchise, which might perhaps not improperly be termed a tenure during good behavior, would in its practical results compare favorably with any." (Report Massachusetts Franchise Committee, 1898.)

Private Control Undesirable. Under private control service is extended and improved only when it becomes highly profitable to effect a change. It is proverbial that "the dividends are in the straps." But, under City control, not merely would promising localities be served in advance of profit—to the greatest possible profit later on; but the older roads in congested districts would be relieved by successive provision for a part of the demands upon them.

Unified Management Desirable under Municipal Control. SECOND—*Combination of concessions is desirable, provided the resulting monopoly is thus made incidentally one of service under City control.*

We have to deal with this situation: The more important existing lines of local transit are held by the syndicate which has secured the subway so far built. The same interest also controls the gas and electrical supply of the city, the future of which largely depends upon the pipe galleries to be constructed in connection with future transit subways. On the one side we have powerful, progressive and intelligent allied corporations in control of the principal public utilities now existing, and on the other side the City, through its power over underground New York, as yet holding this combine at its mercy. For the franchises which it has already granted are insignificant in comparison with those which it still retains, and are dependent upon these latter for their own future profitable operation.

Directly, or through other concessionaries, the City can stimulate competition in all these utilities. Or, by a series of limited short-term grants (with reserved right of resumption), it can control the existing combine; which has most at stake and most to gain by exploitation of new routes.

The City in Command.

The operation of existing franchises can thus be practically dictated. For it is apparent that an electrical, gas and transit alliance, such as exists, can well make greater concessions to the City than any other concern could do; and it will do so about in proportion as the City commands competition. Conversely the City is in a position to demand more and more as its control extends.

It is hard to speak with respect of the claim that New York is so far at the mercy of our great transit combine that extension of its system is our only hope for about seventy-five years to come. This is clearly not true, unless it is to be assumed that it is politically our master. For though the program suggested by the Engineer of our Rapid Transit Commission would place us indefinitely at the mercy of this syndicate, still, as yet, the City of New York controls the situation. With rapidly developing systems capable of independent operation, transfers would be far more vital to the present operating company than to the City. For example—the present Brooklyn Tunnel Extension carries but a single track each way. How could it, or the present Brooklyn surface system, compete with City subways radiating from each end of the Brooklyn Bridge, with this bridge itself used exclusively as a link for the City's new lines? How could private corporations prosper without transfer systems if the same policy were adopted for the Williamsburg, Manhattan and Blackwell's Island bridges, as well as for new and more adequate tunnels under the East and Harlem rivers? Indeed, the City's present advantage is such that it is rather a question of how much the City should demand than what dictation from the present syndicate it should tolerate.

Superficially the City has been exploited in private interest; underground New York is still a virgin plain, not even bounded by the rivers, and under practically complete municipal control.

Underground New York a Virgin Plain.

14

Independent Lines.

THIRD—*It follows that new underground lines should be so planned as to connect with the general system and at the same time constitute continuous systems capable of possible independent operation, which if not accepted by the present operators on the City's terms, could be leased to competitors, or directly operated by the City.*

On Manhattan Island, at least, we believe there is now no north and south line suggested which would not prove immediately profitable.

These undoubtedly profitable lines should be constituted stems of new lines leading to our northerly suburbs—the extremities of which cannot for some years be expected to return a profit on the cost of construction and operation—and crossed by new east and west lines extending from the North river to the eastern boundaries of Queens and Brooklyn. By such procedure the extension of suburban lines will be greatly facilitated.

Objections to Elevated Railways.

FOURTH—*Elevated railroad structures should not be permitted on streets not already disfigured by them except under exceptional conditions.*

Their extension will tend to delay the construction of the City's own subway system in the interest of the privately owned elevated roads and will add obstructions to defer the time when these existing elevated roads, in part at least, should be taken down. For many purposes streets occupied, or localities traversed, by elevated lines are hopelessly disfigured and handicapped. In addition to the cost of construction the City will from now on have to assume the cost of damages to abutting property-owners incident to the construction of elevated railroads. This additional expense will largely increase their cost to an extent comparable with the first cost of underground roads. The earlier plans of the Rapid Transit Commission contemplated "that the streets of New York be dedicated to tunnel railroad purposes." Since the aquisition of the elevated railroads by the Subway Corporation, however, the tentative plans of the Commission indicate a pronounced tendency to extend the present elevated railway systems in all the boroughs and curtail subway construction. Should this policy be finally adopted it will detract greatly from the future beauty and health of the city.*

FIFTH—*For some time to come street tunnels located just below the surface will produce the best results. In the not distant future it will probably be found that a series of deep tunnels to suburban points, with radiates that extend out from congested districts, and not necessarily following street lines, will best serve the purposes of express service.* Shallow and Deep Tunnels.

Experience has demonstrated that either class of tunnels can be built without seriously disturbing travel, and that there is no reason for the people of the city to be again subjected to such grave interference with public and private comforts as has attended the construction of the present subway system.

SIXTH—*Universal transfer in any one general direction within the largest possible one-fare area should be insisted upon.* Transfers.

Bridges—Their Use and Control.

SEVENTH—*The City should forever reserve the fullest control over east and west crosstown connections; feeders, as they should be, for the north and south lines.* Importance of Transverse Lines.

Of these, the four great East river bridges (Brooklyn, Manhattan, Williamsburgh and Blackwell's Island), together with the East and North river tunnels, should be considered essential parts, of which the City should never surrender its exclusive control.

To all intents and purposes and as a consequence of the new bridges and tunnels, New York will ultimately become a square or round city like Chicago or Paris, with the added advantages of cheap independent water transportation for commodities. *These bridges and tunnels are consequently the keys to the successful development of passenger transportation in the interest of the passenger.* Control over them will therefore be eagerly sought by existing transportation companies, whose lines now constitute separate links of a temporary system; which, for New York a Round or Square. Importance of Bridges and Tunnels.

---

* It is not practicable to make new elevated railways independent of existing franchises. This is not true of additional subway lines, which can be made to enlarge the degree of municipal control in contrast to riveting private control by extending the elevated system.

economy and convenience, must soon be welded together. The bridges and river tunnels in New York hold a position analogous to that of the municipal subway in the congested business district of Boston, the control of which by that city enables it to regulate the entire elevated and surface systems which must use the subway.

<small>Terminable Operating License on Brooklyn Bridge.</small>
The existing operating license over the Brooklyn Bridge is an admirable example of a working agreement between the City and its public service companies. The tracks are owned by the City; the railroad corporation pays a fee of five cents per round car trip, and the contract can be abrogated on three months' notice by either party to it. This constitutes what may be termed a limited license to operate as distinguished from a long-term franchise. It tends to place transport corporations continuously under effective municipal control.

<small>Ten-Year Lease, Williamsburgh Bridge.</small>
With this very favorable contract in actual operation and available as a precedent, the Bridge Commissioner has nevertheless entered into a contract for the use of the new Williamsburgh Bridge by the Metropolitan and Brooklyn Rapid Transit Companies, in which he has surrendered the City's position by consenting to a term of ten years, thus abandoning effective control in the interim, and leaving the lessees able to "hold up" during that term any transit plans that involve the use of this bridge.

<small>Correspondence Relating to Same.</small>
Under date of June 6, this committee wrote his Honor the Mayor as follows:

* * * * * * * * *

It is to be noted that while the full term provided for in this contract is ten years, it may nevertheless be terminated by either party on three months' notice, thus placing the matter of surface regulation firmly within the power of the City to control.

In the opinion of this Society, the four East river bridges, which, when completed, will have cost the City upwards of seventy millions of dollars, constitute the great highways of Long Island leading to Manhattan, and their free use for all purposes of municipal travel should be maintained to the utmost practicable extent. It does not seem to us desirable or right that the tracks upon them should be turned over exclusively for so long a period as ten years, as has been done in the case of the Williamsburgh Bridge.

The Bridge Commissioner has stated that the two contracts are similar in their terms, but it does not seem to us that a contract which can be terminated on three months' notice, as is the case with the Brooklyn Bridge contract, is similar to a contract which runs for the full period of ten years without power of termination. The one is a model form of municipal contract, since it leaves the City in control; the other, in comparison, is open to every criticism which can be brought against long-term public-service contracts.

It is true that a large part of Commissioner Best's agreement is composed of provisions seeking to retain large powers of supervision by the City, but in the light of experience no such contractural obligations have proved to be of much avail.

The authority of an appointative official to limit the control of the City over one of its most important bridges for so long a period as attempted in this contract may reasonably be questioned.

The Mayor acknowledged and referred the letter as noted below:

CITY OF NEW YORK—OFFICE OF THE MAYOR.

CALVIN TOMKINS, Esq.,
   National Arts Club,
      No. 37 West Thirty-fourth street, City:

DEAR SIR—The Mayor directs me to acknowledge the receipt of your letter of the 6th instant, and to inform you that it has been transmitted to the Commissioner of Bridges for his prompt attention.

I am
                  Respectfully yours,
                     G. T. GOLDTHWAITE,
                        Assistant Secretary.

The Bridge Commissioner then replied as follows:

DEPARTMENT OF BRIDGES,
CITY OF NEW YORK,
June 23, 1904.

CALVIN TOMKINS, Esq.,
   Chairman, City Plan Committee,
      Municipal Art Society of New York:

DEAR SIR—Your letter of the 6th instant, addressed to the Honorable George B. McClellan, Mayor, is referred to me. When the agreement for operating cars over the Brooklyn Bridge was made, it was entirely tentative and experimental. Neither party knew whether the arrangement would be practicable or advantageous, and I suspect that neither of them believed that it would be advisable to allow the contract to run the full term of ten years. From any other view it would be simply ridiculous to make such a contract, involving the expenditure of so much money in fitting up tracks and have it terminable within three months of the date of the expenditure of the money.

To make an agreement of this character at all attractive to the parties competent to operate it, they should and must be allowed a sufficient time to warrant them in making the effort, and unless the City is prepared to go into the railroad business at any time at short notice, I do not believe in a short-term contract.

Some of the Brooklyn Bridge agreements, notably the one for the use of the docks and right-of-way under the bridge on the Brooklyn side for elevated railroad purposes, were made for twenty years, with the privilege of renewal for a like period.

In my judgment, ten years is the proper term for an agreement such as we are making on the Williamsburgh Bridge. It will take half this time to determine whether the thing will work satisfactorily or not, and the other half will be necessary to enable the City officers to determine what different thing they care to do at the expiration of the lease.

Respectfully yours,
GEORGE E. BEST,
Commissioner of Bridges.

Reply, City Plan Committee.

SEPTEMBER 10, 1904.

Hon. GEO. E. BEST,
Commissioner of Bridges:

DEAR SIR—Your favor of the 23d of June has remained unanswered from the difficulty meanwhile of procuring a full meeting of our committee.

We appreciate that, when the agreement for "operating cars over the Brooklyn Bridge was made, it was entirely tentative and experimental." Now, however, that experience has shown this to have been a most valuable privilege; it seems to us clear that terms more (instead of less) favorable to the City might well have been exacted of the franchise corporations with whom you have contracted for the use of the Williamsburgh Bridge. With universal experience commending retention by the City of the fullest control possible, New York should not have consented to forego such control for ten years to come.

We do not ignore the force of your suggestion that "unless "the City is prepared to go into the railroad business at any time "at short notice I do not believe in a short-term contract." Indeed, this Society believes that power to do this—and such care by its City officials in entering into contracts with private corporations as shall leave New York ever free to exercise such power—constitutes the only protection against extortion by such corporations, and the only basis on which the City can deal with them on equal terms or insure our people a constantly up-to-date service.

We cannot believe your action legal. We know it ought not to be. We know of no limit to the degree to which constant control of the situation is not of advantage to the City. We know of no instance where any surrender of such advantage has not been utilized to the utmost against the public by those to whom it was made.

We therefore submit that you have made a mistake, likely to prove most costly to the City and most profitable to the private interests that seek to exploit public property for private gain.

Very respectfully,
CITY PLAN COMMITTEE,
CALVIN TOMKINS, *Chairman.*

The assumption of the right by the Bridge Commissioner to grant a franchise over the Williamsburg Bridge (if sustained by the courts, which is more than doubtful), leaves the control of passenger transportation over the bridges with the following authorities: Diverse Authority Over Bridges.

1st. The Mayor and Board of Aldermen under the general charter provisions over franchises.

2d. The State Rapid Transit Commission, as the result of legislation at their request, granted last winter.

3d. The Bridge Commissioner, by assumption.

This state of affairs is unfortunate considering the delicate and complicated nature of the principles involved. The four bridges will be the great highways between Long Island and Manhattan Island. They will have been constructed at large expense by the City, and their greatest potential usefulness should be availed of by the community and not diverted to the special advantage of a few favored public service corporations.

20

<small>Great Responsibility Rapid Transit Commission.</small> The responsibility of the Rapid Transit Commission in this matter is complete—as a consequence of the action of the last legislature in granting them this degree of control at their own request.

East River Bridge Connections.

<small>The Bridges as Public Highways.</small> In the use of the bridges for passenger traffic they should also be considered exclusively as surface streets (of which they are all too limited a continuation across the river) normally to be used only for surface traffic and connections. This would leave sub-river subway connections to be made by tunnel under the river, that is, the bridges, the City's property, would be reserved for more strictly street uses, and private subway contractors left to provide their own sub-river connections. Later, municipal subways, as well, should be similarly planned as parts of an underground system—reaching from the Orange Mountains on the west to Nassau on the east, and from Yonkers, Mount Vernon and New Rochelle on the north, under Richmond to Perth Amboy on the south. Such subways would not be restricted by street lines—while the surface streets, including the bridges, would be kept for strictly surface traffic. This would not interfere with the temporary use (by the City itself) of the bridges, *its own* property, for municipal and subway connections which could later be provided for by tunnel, as indicated.

<small>Collecting and Diffusing Bridge Passengers in Manhattan.</small> The following extracts from a letter by Bridge Commissioner George E. Best, relative to the Manhattan extension of the East River bridges, while differing as regards routes, elevated structures and necessity for bridge connections from the suggestions of this Society, are pertinent to the present discussion and indicative of the growing official tendency to regard the bridges as street extensions:

SEPTEMBER 7, 1904.
The Hon. GEO. B. MCCLELLAN,
   Mayor of New York City:

DEAR SIR—It is of the utmost importance to the boroughs of Brooklyn and Queens, and to the welfare of the City of New York, that more liberal and better facilities shall be furnished for railway travel over the East river. It is not enough that bridges of great capacity shall be built over the river, means must be devised and methods adopted for the collection and diffusion of passengers to and from these bridges.   *   *   *

No provision has yet been made for the diffusion of the masses of people who now cross the old bridge and who will soon cross the new bridge away from the City Hall station and away from Clinton and Delancey streets, where great crowds will soon be landed at a point far from the destination which they desire.

The much-talked of bridge connecting railways would, to an extent, prevent congestion of cars and people at the bridge terminals, but none of the routes proposed for these railways traverse or reach districts of greatest travel, and while cars crossing from Brooklyn might be speedily returned by the routes already proposed, nothing like a maximum efficiency of distribution of travel would be accomplished by their use.   *   *   *

In order that the experience on the Williamsburgh Bridge may not be repeated and that the Manhattan Bridge may afford at once when finished the relief which its completion promises, lines of railway away from it and to connect with up and down town railways now existing should be determined upon and constructed.   *   *   *

In view of the above, I venture to suggest for your consideration and for such action as may seem to be best the following routes for railways, which should, in my judgment, be in substance provided at the earliest practicable date.

1st. An elevated railway through Canal street, from Greenwich street or the Hudson river to the Manhattan Bridge terminal, with a branch through Elm street, Centre street, or the Bowery to Delancey street, and through this street to the terminus of the Williamsburgh Bridge.   *   *   *

2d. A trolley subway through Delancey street, the Bowery and Spring street, across town to Hudson street, down Hudson street, West Broadway and Greenwich street, at least as far as the Jersey City ferries at Cortlandt and Liberty streets, with a branch through Duane street, under the present subway at Elm street, into the basement of the projected station on Centre street, there to connect with the trolley lines from Brooklyn, which could use the basement of this station as a terminal and through station.

This line might be built and operated either by the Brooklyn trolley companies, as an extension of their line into the rich feeding ground of Manhattan, or by the Jersey City railway companies, who will shortly cross the Hudson river to Manhattan by tunnel, and who would, I believe, be glad to avail themselves of this means of rapid and safe connection with two of the Broovlyn bridges. This route between the Williamsburgh and Brooklyn bridges need not be operated as a loop or connecting railway, although this is quite possible, but cars could be operated from the Williamsburgh Bridge to some point on Hudson street or to the Jersey City ferries and return, and the cars over the Brooklyn Bridge could be operated in the same manner, or the Jersey City cars could be operated to the ferry and bridge terminals and receive passengers at these points and at intermediate stations for Jersey City. * * *

Respectfully,

G. E. BEST,

Commissioner of Bridges.

<small>No Bridge Terminals.</small> This Committee believes there should be no distinctively "bridge terminals," and submits its conclusions as follows:

Between Manhattan and The Bronx there is a bridge at which focuses the east side rapid transit traffic of both boroughs. We never hear of fighting crowds at either end; we have never been bothered about the connections which the traffic over it makes with the routes to the north and south.

Between Manhattan and Brooklyn we have one bridge long in use, another ready, and another building. In the case of the first the crush at its Manhattan terminal is a danger and scandal, and its relation to Manhattan traffic a problem ever more acute. Similar conditions are assumed as probable at the Manhattan ends of the "Williamsburg" and "Manhattan" bridges, unless we meanwhile find a way out—in each case the only serious trouble being at the western end.

It is true that, within a thousand feet of the Park row end of the present Brooklyn Bridge is located the daily work of so many who arrive by it that a station there might always be a fairly busy one. But the great mass of those who arrive in Manhattan by the Brooklyn Bridge are dumped out at Park Row, far from their destination or from any connection by which they can get to it.

<small>Cause Bridge Crush.</small> What, then, is it that turns into pandemonium at City Hall Park conditions everywhere else too well handled to be other

than commonplace? It is this, and this only: In the sense that it is so adjusted as to create congestion the Park Row bridge station (*one end* of a single bridge) is our only bridge " terminal "; and, at that, it is one too many. As a factor of a transport system a bridge should have *no* " terminals," but should be simply the section of a continuous route that happens to be carried over water. There is no more excuse for dumping all psssengers at Park Row than there would be for putting them all out at any single point in Brooklyn, to dodge about on foot in the weather. There is no reason why all Bridge cars should not go west to the North river, as well as east to Long Island destinations; no reason why a Manhattan passenger should not be able to transfer to or from a Bridge car at Broadway, West Broadway and West street, as well as Park Row, and thus connect with every north and south line in Manhattan and with Jersey City ferries and tunnels as well.

If bridge traffic needs loop facilities, congestion might be avoided and public interest better accommodated by sending west bound cars to West street by some cross street a few blocks north of the Bridge, then southward along West street and back eastward a few blocks south of the bridge (the direct westerly approach to the bridge underground through City Hall Park being temporarily sealed by the line of the first subway, as noted on page 7). Remedy

Why has such a plan not been followed here? *It has repeatedly been followed, but only in cases where the one who arranged matters was so inspired by private interest that he could see beyond the end of the Bridge.* When the Brooklyn Bridge was first opened, our City officials standing upon it saw beyond neither end of it, and we had Bridge cars—*without connections at either end.* Later " Brooklyn Rapid Transit " has been given possession, and since the B. R. T. depends on Brooklyn connections, the Bridge has them. The B. R. T. does not control Manhattan connections, so the Bridge dumps it passengers at Park Row. The " Metropolitan " aggregation of Manhattan swallowed the Bronx system. That insured that its passengers should not be discharged with an "All out " at either end of its Harlem Bridge. Private Interest.

Rivalry of Transit Corporations.

If either company or the Belmont interest owned the Brooklyn Bridge, it would long since have used this advantage to develop routes from the North river to the eastern line of Queens, and have dictated connections with every north and south line that crossed them. But since it is only the City that owns the bridges —and the streets, subsoil as well as surface, at both ends of each, and the Rapid Transit Commission has been constituted by the State to do the City's thinking—the City looks distractedly at present conditions, as might a man on whose lawn rival contractors were fighting to settle how they should adjust his premises at his expense.

Bridge Connections not Needed.

Current "plans" involve either a subway or an elevated structure *connecting the Manhattan ends* of the two bridges (" Brooklyn " and " Williamsburg "). What for? What reason is there to think that more people want to go from one bridge to the other than wish to travel between City Hall Park and any other place as far out of the way as the junction of Suffolk and Delancey streets? Why not continue the trains from each bridge to where passengers do want to go? Or to connections that will most promptly land them there? The answer is one that he who runs may be read. It is assumed that the Metropolitan system will fight any continuation of Brookyln lines into Manhattan; that the B. R. T. would collapse if it were turned off the Bridge and the Metropolitan allowed to establish rapid transit facilities from all Manhattan to our eastern suburbs; that the Belmont interest insists that each new factor be made such a mere extension of its route so that no other contractor can bid; and, finally, that the City has no rights—though it owns the bridges and the streets, and must pay for building the lines, and its citizens are to use them.

The situation is an embarrassing one—if all that the City has to do is apportion its rights between private undertakers. But it is a clear one—so clear that if longer muddled by failure to vindicate the City's interests it will neither be forgotten nor pardoned by our people.

What should be done? Just what, if the "Metropolitan" or Comprehensive
the B. R. T. or the Belmont interest had owned what the City now Transit Plan
owns, either would long since have done. A comprehensive plan Needed
should be devised for rapid transit throughout the city; not for
complete realization at once, but that each step may be taken
with intelligent reference to the end in view. Any contractor,
corporate or individual, could then bid for any portion with
regard to its relation to the whole—already fixed in the public
interest. But until such plan exists, the adoption of any proposition—however well intentioned or well worked out by itself—
must almost necessarily embarrass future development.

Such a plan should be devised with little or no regard to opera- Existing
tion by present franchise corporations. So far as concerns their Corporations to Conform
systems, these are so obsolete and inadequate, and would be so Service to
dependent for profitable operation on transfer and other con- Same.
nections with the new lines, that for the City to wait for them or
yield to their defiance would be to lose dollars to save cents, and
be mulcted for generations to gain a few months now. Within
twenty years—largely within ten—there will be left worth consideration (except as incidentals) but little of our present surface
and elevated systems. The idea of our present franchise corporations venturing a real struggle with the one power that can
parallel at cost—without watering stock—every facility they can
offer, is preposterous. On the contrary, if the City insists, they
will be glad to serve it on its own terms; and when these are
settled, they may well prove our very best agents to operate a
large part of our developing system.

So far, however, as concerns the semi-daily melee at Park
Row, and the use of Williamsburg Bridge, and assuming that
details now suggested must be checked by the general plan into
which they are fit, the following may illustrate the suggestions
already made.

At the Brooklyn Bridge: With the exception of the few Present
who transfer from the Bridge to the Third avenue elevated, or Inconvenience.
Third and Fourth avenue surface cars, confused connections with
which are here made, all Bridge passengers are landed in Park
Row and sent across its easterly sidewalk tramping toward their

destinations, or (from 500 to 1,500 feet) through a maze of traffic to their Broadway, West Broadway, Greenwich street or West street connections, thus compelling all who travel by the Bridge to rendezvous at its entrance—the comers every morning, the goers every evening—into such a mob as cannot be matched.

Brooklyn Bridge Crosstown Exten-ion.
Suppose that, instead of the present plan, the north or Manhattan bound tracks were continued by a curve to the north in descending subway to opposite Reade and Elm streets; thence passed under the present subway and across under Reade to West street; then under West to Liberty; then under Liberty and the Broadway subway to Nassau; then under Nassau and the east side of Park Row back to and over the Bridge as its southern tracks; with stations say at Reade and Broadway, Reade and West Broadway, West and Warren, West and Barclay, West and Liberty and Liberty and Nassau streets. (See Plate B.)

There would be no jam at Park Row beyond such as is now handled at the Rector or Cortlandt street elevated stations. Those who transferred to or from the Third avenue elevated, or the Third or Fourth avenue surface cars, would do so direct by stairs instead of walking as far as now. The comparatively few to whom the Park Row station is most convenient would embark there without even crowding the sidewalks. Every one else would remain in the cars until he reached the one of the half dozen widely distributed new stations proposed, to which again he would go when he wished to return. Every one would be convenienced; Bridge traffic eased by a practicable "loop"; the present crush split into half a dozen ordinary station concourses; and, *as must soon become equally important,* the sidewalk space used twice a day by each Bridge passenger greatly reduced—thus relieving, as well as distributing, present lower Manhattan congestion.

If it be said that the east side connection at Park Row (surface and elevated) calls for additional facilities from that point eastward, a part or all of the centre cars connecting with the Brooklyn Bridge elevated routes might be reserved for this, with transfers from other cars to them at that point. If both express

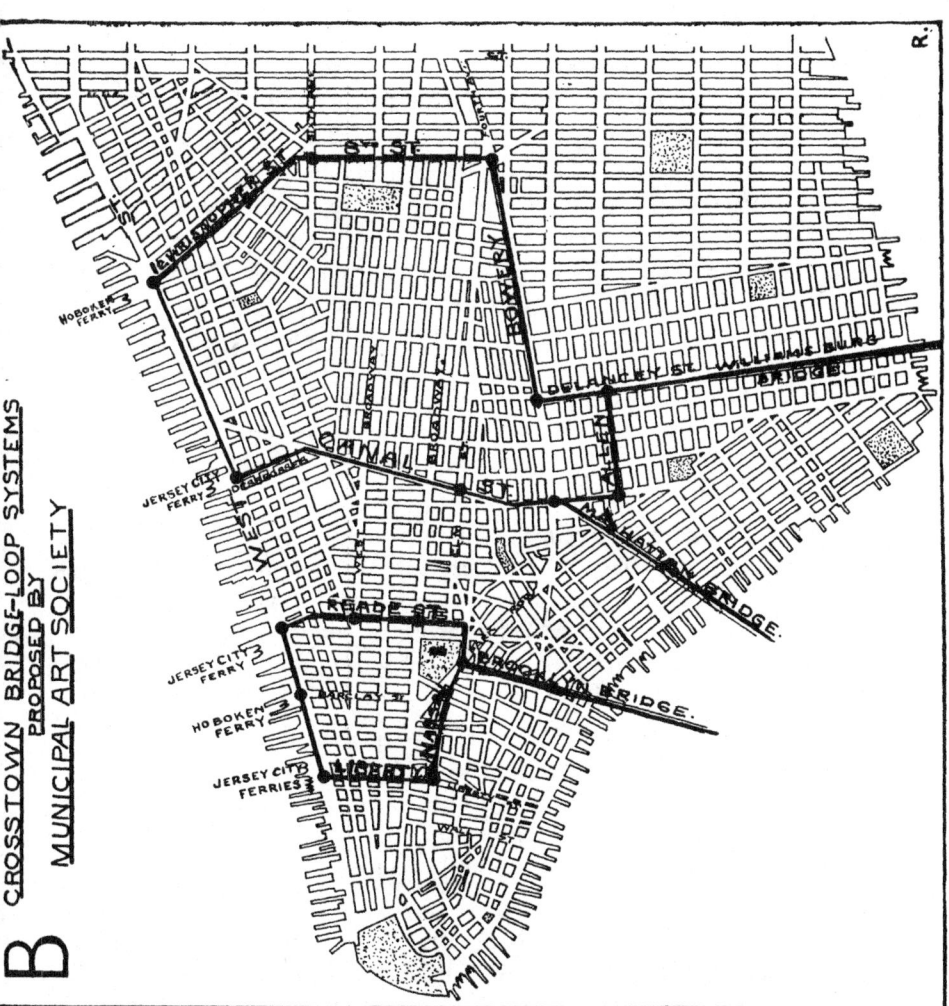

and local service across Manhattan are to be provided for, one of these could be given by the outer pair of Bridge tracks and the other by the inner pair, and the northerly tracks of each (side by side or one above the other) sent around the West street loop to return as the southerly track of each. One extra "express" station, say at Barclay and West streets, would be all that would be needed on the loop, and, with one at the Bridge entrance, would well connect Brooklyn with Jersey City ferries (and tunnels to be), as well as with the north and south lines on each side of Manhattan.

As to room, there is plenty of it, the most critical point being at Park Row, where the present subway (not planned for such a case), might obstruct direct continuance to or beyond Broadway. But by subway on declining grade under the east side of Park Row there would be as little trouble in getting under the present subway at Reade street as there would be (after coming back under it at Broadway and Liberty street) in getting back to the Bridge again by ascending curve from the south. As to minor obstacles: This plan solves the greater problem. No comparitively petty interest, public or private, should be permitted to thwart it.

Avoidance Crosstown Elevated Systems

Of alternatives suggested, it is safe to say that whatever may be proposed, the City will never actually permit such defacement as would be an elevated structure connecting the bridges; certainly not with the added expense of condemnation through the blocks; least of all as a trestle of wrought iron junk stretching from Park Row to or across Broadway.

A better reason, however, why neither an elevated nor a subway connection between the bridges should be constructed is that it is not merely the worst way to make the loop, but *it leaves the Bridge crush still unsolved;* and is defensible only on the assumption that the chief end of rapid transit is a dividend for the B. R. T.

Williamsburgh Bridge Crosstown Extension.

As to the Williamsburg Bridge, the case is similar, except that it reaches grade at Suffolk and Delancey streets, where few connections focus, and where fewest would normally want to land or start. Moreover, Delancey street is already widened westward. Not to repeat suggestions such as have already been made, the following is a " for example " of what might be done here: The loop route of the north or west bound tracks might be: From the junction of Allen and Delancey streets; under Delancey to the Bowery; under Bowery to Eighth; under Eighth (and Clinton place) to Christopher; under Christopher to West; under West to Desbrosses; under Desbrosses and Canal to Allen; under Allen and back to Bridge entrance; with stations at Bowery and Delancey, Cooper Union, Sixth avenue and Eighth street, Christopher and West, Desbrosses and West, and Canal and Elm, and Bowery and Canal—thus connecting with the great north and south lines, as well as Jersey City ferries and tunnel. (See Plate B.)

Other connections should be facilitated, such as one (with through cars) at Cooper Union with the present subway, so vital to the latter that the City, not it, would be dictator. Again, the southerly curve of the loop practically touches the proposed landing of the Manhattan Bridge, now building. And to other West street connections would soon be added the river front " elevated " that is sure to come.

It is assumed that from the Brooklyn ends of each of these bridges diverging subways will ultimately be extended to the eastern suburbs, and that meanwhile full control of the bridges will be kept in the City by every precaution, including short leases, with option to the City of resumption, so that any arrangement with present franchise corporations cannot be later used by them to thwart the City's interest. (See Plate C.) _{Provision for Brooklyn Radiating Systems of Subways.}

In any loop plan, the question of extent of divergence between the hither and thither tracks is a question of balancing convenience little affecting the principle. For example: As to each bridge, one could be worked out in its essentials by a single street connection across the island for both east and west tracks, with the loop only at West street, which is amply wide for the purpose, especially if the tracks commenced to diverge just before reaching it.

The foregoing are merely illustrations, and could doubtless be bettered. Their " moral " is:

(1) *Whatever one or another of our franchise corporations may want,* the City has no special need for either elevated or

subway connection between its bridge terminals in Manhattan; and the way to treat the present problem of danger and riot is radically to better present conditions in the way best calculated to serve our people, leaving each and every franchise corporation to make the best of that result; and

<small>Bridges are Trunk Sections of Continuous Streets.</small> (2) A bridge should not be considered as an isolated structure, but simply as a "trunk" section of continuous streets reaching every locality of the city; hence, for transit purposes, involving no special scheme of "terminals" whatever.*

A Comprehensive Plan.

EIGHTH—*The City should promptly plan and begin to build a comprehensive transit system.*

<small>Urgency for Planning a Comprehensive System.</small> It does not seem to this Committee that the Rapid Transit Commission has been sufficiently prompt or explicit in this regard. Fairness to the multifarious private interests in the city, as well as the direct interest of the citizens at large, demands prompt and definite settlement of the general plan. The system should be planned with reference, not so much to the greatest immediate profit to be derived from the construction of new lines as with a view to the relief of congested districts by a shifting of population, and of adequately connecting the outlying boroughs with the central parts of the city. It would also soon come to exercise so comprehensive and dominating an influence over all public utility grants, past, present and future, as to place the City in an ever stronger position of control.

---

* Though our Committee's intent has been simply to present the essential principal which it feels has been too long ignored, and it has therefore not gone into side issues, it notes that whatever the merits of other plans proposed, ours could be so adjusted as to include them, e. g.

1. Though we disapprove of further elevated structures our plan would in some respect be facilitated by them.

2. Though we do not agree with those who have considered connection of each bridge with the others as a specially crying need, the loops proposed could easily be so arranged as to effect this.

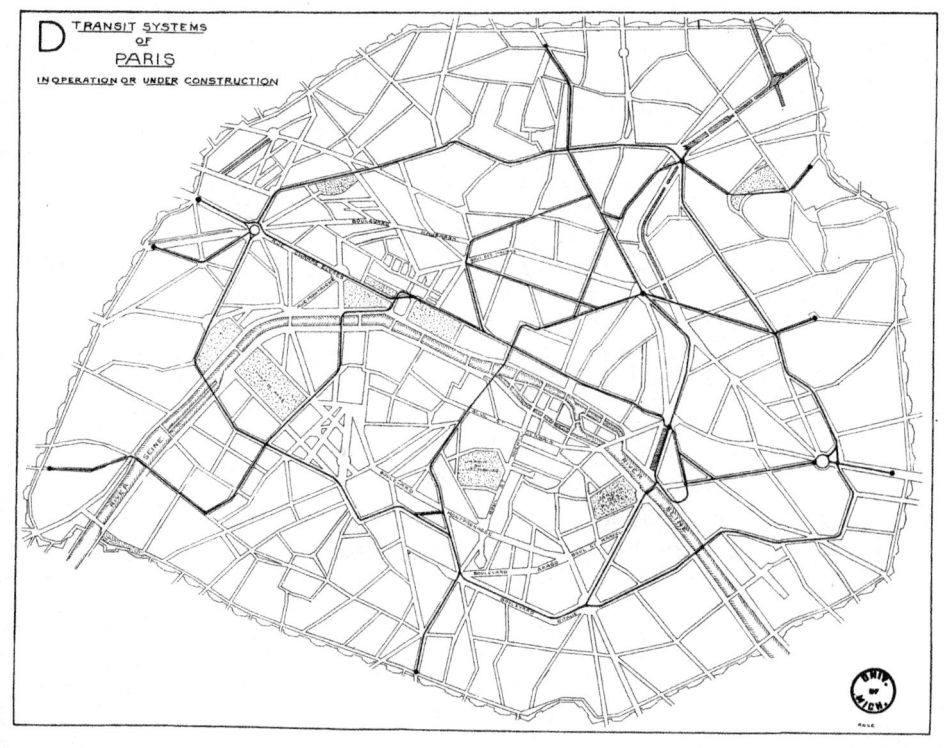

A plan of the Paris subway system is appended (Plate D) as indicative of what should be provided here; part of this Paris system is in operation; part is under construction and part exists only on the published plans, but the general scheme in its entirety has been clearly laid before the people of the city and as individuals they are placed in a position to adapt themselves to future conditions. As indicative of the popular sense of doubt, distrust and conjecture which exists here, we quote from the conservative real estate paper of the city as follows: Paris Subway Plan.

These reports of consolidation are very vague, and we do not make mention of them because of their value as news, but because they constitute a peculiarly good illustration of the obscurity in which the ultimate purposes of the private capitalists who control the rapid transit of Greater New York are shrouded, and the doubt as to the identity of the men who do and will exercise that control. Thus, the reporters have it that somehow the Whitney-Widener-Elkins group of street railway financiers are bringing about this new consolidation; that they really control the Interborough Rapid Transit Co.; that the Brooklyn Rapid Transit can be taken over whenever they please, and that the Pennsylvania Railroad and interests connected with it are at bottom the chief influences in the syndicate. What the reports all point to is an immense consolidation of the rapid transit interests of Long Island, Hudson and Essex counties in New Jersey, and New York County in the hands of the Pennsylvania Railroad and its auxiliaries. Now, this report is probably the greatest nonsense in the world; but no better example could be asked of the possible aims of what may be called the secret financial diplomacy of the rich capitalists. What is true and significant is the fact that a few of these men, through the control they exercise of certain big corporations, can in effect reach secret agreements, vitally affecting the welfare of the 5,000,000 people resident in the territory above described without giving any of these 5,000,000 people or their official representatives a chance to be consulted. Whatever we may think of the means taken to accomplish these ends, there can be no doubt that the feeling of distrust and the desire for authentic statements of facts is well justified and will have to be reckoned with hereafter by the big men.—*N. Y Record and Guide,* Aug. 8, 1903. Doubt, Distrust, Conjecture.

This principle—of a comprehensive plan—is a vital one, constantly to be kept in mind in passing on such suggestions as that for the extension of a Hudson river tunnel through Christopher street and up Sixth avenue—thus ruining that avenue for a system of through subway lines running north and south if placed near the surface; or for a system of east and west crosstown lines if Comprehensive Sixth Avenue Route and Crosstown System.

placed at a lower level, as now proposed by the New Jersey corporation. The Fourteenth street, Twenty-third street and Thirty-fourth street crosstown lines are most urgently needed, and their construction should not be interfered with by a subway dam along Sixth avenue. The construction of the bridges and tunnels over and under the rivers implies the rapid lateral development of the city, for which provision should now be made, and the Sixth avenue system proposed by the New York and New Jersey Tunnel Company should not be permitted until such time as the City's own gridiron subway and transfer system shall have been definitely planned, otherwise serious complications will surely arise. Again, the City should be careful how it extends local transit privileges in its streets to New Jersey transport companies. It is most important that every facility should be extended to lines traversing the Metropolitan District of New Jersey that are extended to Long Island lines, but the utmost care should be taken that a like degree of municipal control shall be maintained over all. Indeed, somewhat of delay in urgently needed facilities should be suffered rather than go further with piecemeal provision, in advance of settlement of a general plan to which such local details could then be adjusted.

New Jersey and Long Island Routes.

Traffic from New Jersey by tunnel should be taken directly across the island of Manhattan and to Long Island suburbs by our East river bridges and tunnels, and then returned by loops through the same or parallel streets to the Hudson river tunnels. Conversely, bridge and tunnel traffic from Long Island boroughs should be conducted, as far as practicable, through these same tunnels to the North river. Transfers north and south in Manhattan over north and south municipal lines should be provided at street intersections, and a limited number of through trains between New Jersey and Long Island points ultimately arranged for.

Manhattan Transfers.

Example Pennsylvania Railroad Tunnel.

For a limited strip the Pennsylvania Railroad Company's tunnel will accomplish this when completed; and the City should not be less farsighted in providing for its own future welfare.

New York Connecting Railroad.

In this connection the local traffic agreement now proposed by the Rapid Transit Commission for the control of traffic over the intended Pennsylvania Railroad line running through Brooklyn from Bay Ridge to Astoria, and thence by bridge* over Randall's and Ward's Islands to the Bronx, where it will connect with the New York, New Haven and Hartford system, is open to criticism in that it defines local traffic (as distinguished from through traffic over which the City exerts no control) to include only the carriage of passengers and freight between points all within the boroughs of Brooklyn and Queens, and between points all within the Borough of The Bronx—thus contravening the principle laid down by the Rapid Transit Board itself (page 13, Report 1902). " The policy and intention of the Board are to the very utmost that is practicable to require every contractor for the construction and operation of a municipal railroad to stipulate to make fair operating arrangements upon the basis of a single fare for a single trip over any or all other municipally constructed railroads."

Whatever be the force of the " continuing line, one fare " argument, it is scarcely consistent for the Commission to waive in favor of the Pennsylvania Railroad the very principle upon which the Commission has excused its leanings toward confirming the Belmont Syndicate in monopoly of rapid transit extension on the ground (mistaken), that thus alone could that principle be carried out. If the Commission do not consider the local traffic of this company as being in any sense "municipal," they might at least provide for a single fare between the boroughs, as was done in the case of the Pennsylvania's tunnel crossing from Manhattan to Long Island.

The following extract from the Report of O. F. Nichols, the Chief Engineer of the Bridge Department, to Bridge Commissioner G. F. Best, under date of March 9, 1904, deserves especial consideration as embodying the essential principle which should control the use of a railroad connecting the Manhattan ends of the bridges.

" It would be extremely unwise to tie the connecting railway up to any definite system for so long a period without the possibility of change or readjustment, when we know that the condi- City Shoul Control Bridge Co necting Sul ways.

---

* The best site for a bridge to connect Queens and The Bronx has been devoted to a bridge for railroad purposes exclusively, when a combined general traffic and railroad bridge might have been as readily arranged for.

tions in Brooklyn are such as to require readjustment perhaps within three to five years from the completion of the connection.

" Whichever plan for a connecting railway is adopted, it should be built under provisions specifically exempting it from the limiting conditions of the Rapid Transit Act, as to terms of lease, or indeed from the similar conditions of chapter 712 of the Laws of 1901. The connecting railway should be as free in this respect as the Brooklyn and Williamsburg bridges with which it connects, and any legislation on the subject which may hereafter be procured should place the three bridges and the railways connecting them precisely in the same condition for use or lease, to the end that these structures shall not be tied up in a conflicting manner, but be left so free that the leaseholds may be made sufficiently brief to provide for changes in operation corresponding with the changes in conditions of the public requirements."

<small>Basis for Planning Manhattan East Side and Long Island Routes.</small>

As before noted, this committee sees no necessity *per se* for connecting the several East river bridges at the Manhattan ends, but the suggestion of Engineer Nichols affords the basis for planning a new independent trunk subway system leading to The Bronx, with extensions to Kings and Queens boroughs and up the west side of Manhattan.

Considering such bridge connecting subway as a stem line, the following suggestions were submitted by this committee to the Rapid Transit Commission, May 12, 1904:

MAY 12, 1904.

<small>Letter Municipal Art Society to Rapid Transit Commission.</small>

To the Honorable the Rapid Transit Commission of the City of New York:

GENTLEMEN—In a recent report of your honorable body, the statement is made that routes now adopted should be so designed as to meet present demonstrated demands, rather than to anticipate the needs of the future. In this connection we would respectfully call your attention to the fact that the most congested parts of Manhattan, east of the Bowery and extending along the East river—and along the Hudson as well—do not seem to have been considered in planning new subways. However much needed the routes at present outlined may be, we believe that congestion of traffic on existing lines can best be relieved and the interests of the city best served by now draining these densely populated areas of their excess population by way of the Williamsburg Bridge to the boroughs of Queens and Brooklyn. When completed, the Manhattan and Blackwell's

Island bridges should be promptly availed of as well. (See Plate C.) Examination of the carefully prepared maps of the Tenement House Commission, which show the relative density of population, considered in connection with the accelerating movement of population from Manhattan to Brownsville and other parts of the above mentioned boroughs, alike indicate the immediate practical necessity for transit routes over the bridges to the outskirts of Queens and Brooklyn.

The development of a well-devised system of bridge connections by means of a capacious East Side subway, ultimately designed to connect with the entrances of the Brooklyn, Manhattan, Williamsburg and Blackwell's Island bridges, should be planned for now; and as each bridge is completed should be made effective without delay. Such a subway should be utilized as the bridges are now utilized and doubtless will continue to be, *i. e.*, not exclusively by one company, under a long term lease, but by means of short term licenses to operate, granted to more than one operating company at the same time over the same line. Such a license, we understand, is now in vogue on the Brooklyn Bridge, and is terminable either by the City or the licensees on short notice. Service by this means can be kept under effective municipal control. Such an East Side subway, extending southward from the Yonkers line through The Bronx, across the Harlem, through the densely populated section near the East river, connecting on its way with each of the East river bridges, then running westward via City Hall, or Battery, or both, and then proceeding northward, keeping near the North river and through the populous districts of the West Side to, say, Seventy-second street, thence crossing eastward to the east route above described—would, in our judgment, best serve the purposes of local transportation in Manhattan and of through transportation to the outskirts of The Bronx, Brooklyn and Queens; at the same time its construction would constitute a perfectly safe and conservative investment for the City. {Bronx and Brooklyn Served, Manhattan Congestion Relieved.}

Respectfully submitted,

CALVIN TOMKINS,

President, the Municipal Art Society of New York.

The construction and short-term leasing of such a line (see Plate A) in Manhattan and The Bronx, with trunk line extensions over the bridges to Kings and Queens (see Plate C) ; the additional construction of immediately profitable crosstown subways {An Independent, Profitable, Desirable System.}

36

such as those noted on Plates A and B, and with full municipal control reserved over other important transverse street and over the bridges as well, would place the City in a dominating position of control over all transportation companies within its boundaries, and accomplish this without risk to its credit, and without any undue financial strain upon its resources. Its operation would be profitable from the start.

Avoid a Dependent System.

This Committee cannot but infer that the suggestions made to the Rapid Transit Commission and to the Bridge Commissioner for deflecting the course of Brooklyn Bridge traffic to the north at the proposed Centre street terminal, coupled with the suggestions for connecting the bridges, have for their ultimate object a series of bridge loops in the interest of the Brooklyn Rapid Transit Company and the initiation of a new *dependent* north and south subway or elevated line in Manhattan following the general route above described, to be controlled by the Interborough Company. We agree in thinking that such a subway (not elevated) line should be promptly planned and built. But it should be constituted a line capable of *independent* operation, and under a larger degree of municipal control than any so far constructed, and it should not *increase* congestion by terminating at the Brooklyn Bridge entrance.

Rapid Transit Commission Plans.

Rapid Transit Commission Plans.

In its previous Transit Bulletin (1903) the Society discussed at length the prospective plans of the Rapid Transit Commission as they were then set forth, and also offered detailed suggestions for other routes. (This Bulletin, No. 3, can be obtained on application to the Secretary of the Society.) How far the earlier plans of the Commission are still being considered and to precisely what extent they have been modified by later developments we cannot judge. We do understand, however, that the Commission has since passed the Pennsylvania Railroad plans for a belt line through Brooklyn and for an extension of the Flatbush avenue subway line through Ocean avenue to the tracks of the Brighton Beach Railway, also for the Hudson and Manhattan

Tunnel under the river and along Cortlandt, Fulton and Church streets.

The first two projects are now before the Board of Aldermen for their action, and the latter has been approved by that body.

In addition, the Commission refer to their Engineer's report on the following routes, without definite commitment, however, on their part:

A Manhattan subway system, north bound from Forty-second street on the east side, and south bound from Forty-second street on the west side. This system is partly planned in the interest of the New York City Railway Company and partly in the interest of the Interborough Company.

An extension of the Brooklyn subway system from Atlantic avenue along Fourth avenue to Fort Hamilton and from the Park Plaza along the Eastern parkway to East New York avenue; also a river tunnel from Atlantic avenue to Whitehall.

A tunnel by way of Orange and Nassau streets, Brooklyn, under the East river, Maiden lane, William street, Brooklyn Bridge entrance, Centre street, Grand street, Delancey street, and thence connecting with the elevated system of that bridge and subsequently with the Manhattan Bridge as well.

Suggestions for elevated roads along the Southern Boulevard, Boston road and Jerome avenue in The Bronx.

An extension of the New York Central tracks by an elevated structure along Eleventh avenue and West street to the Battery.

An extension of the Second avenue elevated tracks across Blackwell's Island Bridge into Queens and across the Williamsburgh Bridge into Brooklyn.

An increased number of tracks on the Second, Third and Ninth avenue elevated roads in Manhattan and the extension of the Sixth avenue elevated through Christopher street to Greenwich street.

"An extensive development of the Brooklyn Rapid Transit elevated system in various directions."

An extension of the Brooklyn elevated railroad system over the several East river bridges, into and through the streets of

Manhattan, with connections between the Manhattan ends of these bridges by similar elevated railway structures. As above noted, it is impossible to determine to what extent the above suggestions of the Rapid Transit Commission are likely to be carried out, or to what extent they have already been modified by the Commission itself. Their very existence tends to accentuate the desirability of the adoption of a comprehensive, well articulated subway transit plan, which shall admit of elevated structures only under urgent and peculiar conditions.

Municipal Art Society's Plans.

<small>Detailed Plan for Manhattan North and South Lines.</small>

The shape of Manhattan and its density of population strain the carrying capacity of north and south lines. On each side of the city near the river and for several blocks back the population is most dense (see notes showing relative density of population, as recently published by the Tenement House Commission). To serve the greatest number of people, and to relieve congestion on other lines, an additional subway should be at once constructed here, and could be favorably leased at once. For this reason we recommend that on Manhattan Island the following loop subway should first be constructed: From the city line down Jerome avenue in The Bronx, crossing the Harlem by tunnel to Seventh avenue, thence to One Hundred and Twenty-fifth street, there dividing, one line going west and down Amsterdam avenue, Tenth avenue, Fourteenth street, Hudson street, Chambers street, Park Row, Bowery, Canal, Allen street, First avenue, One Hundred and Twenty-fifth street to junction at Seventh avenue. (See Plate A.)

<small>Battery Extension.</small>

We also suggest an extension of the above system from Chambers street, through West Broadway, Greenwich street, under and around the Battery; thence, by reason of narrow streets,

---

* Further than indicating the general purposes which should control the tunnel approaches to New York from New Jersey, this report does not discuss the development of the transit problem in connection with that State. For economic and social considerations these northern counties of New Jersey constitute an integral part of the municipal area, and should be so considered, and their interests should be harmonized in a comprehensive plan with those of New York.

dividing into two subways, one through Pearl street and New Bowery, joining the main system at Chatham Square, the other through Water street and Catharine street, joining the main line at the same point (see Plate A).

At Fourteenth street, the widest part of Manhattan, there are but twelve possible north and south avenues available for subways; and below Fourteenth street still fewer subway opportunities exist. These should be husbanded to the utmost potential capacity of each street. Again, all the principal crosstown streets connecting the East river bridges, ferries, tunnels and other important points with those on the North river, will be required for a system of lower level crosstown subways from the west side of Manhattan (or from New Jersey) across Manhattan to the Queens boundary. Limited Number of Possible Manhattan Routes.

Crosstown subway connections on Manhattan are suggested at Fourteenth street, Twenty-third street, Thirty-fourth street, Fifty-ninth street, Seventy-second street, Eighty-sixth street and One Hundred and Tenth street (see Plate A). Transverse connections farther south from the Brooklyn, Manhattan and Williamsburgh bridges are for greater clearness shown on a separate plate (B). East and West Manhattan Lines.

The construction of the main west side tunnel and crosstown connections above Thirty-fourth street might be deferred until such time as the existing west side tunnel shall prove to be inadequate, the great necessity for rapid transit at the present time being relief for the crowded east side and for an east side Bronx express service. Defer West Side Construction.

Plate F indicates the general north and south trend of travel on the narrow Island of Manhattan and the radial direction of passenger distribution in semi-circular Brooklyn. This is the situation which exists at every bridge crossing between Manhattan and Brooklyn. Brooklyn System.

" Scarcely less difficult than the transportation problem of Manhattan is that of Brooklyn with its fan-like shape and narrow, congested streets. Its long main lines of traffic tend toward and converge at a few strategic points along its water front, where the business districts are located or where there are outlets by bridge or ferries to Manhattan. Brooklyn's chief transportation problem is not merely to move its population to its own business district, but to move a considerable proportion of the

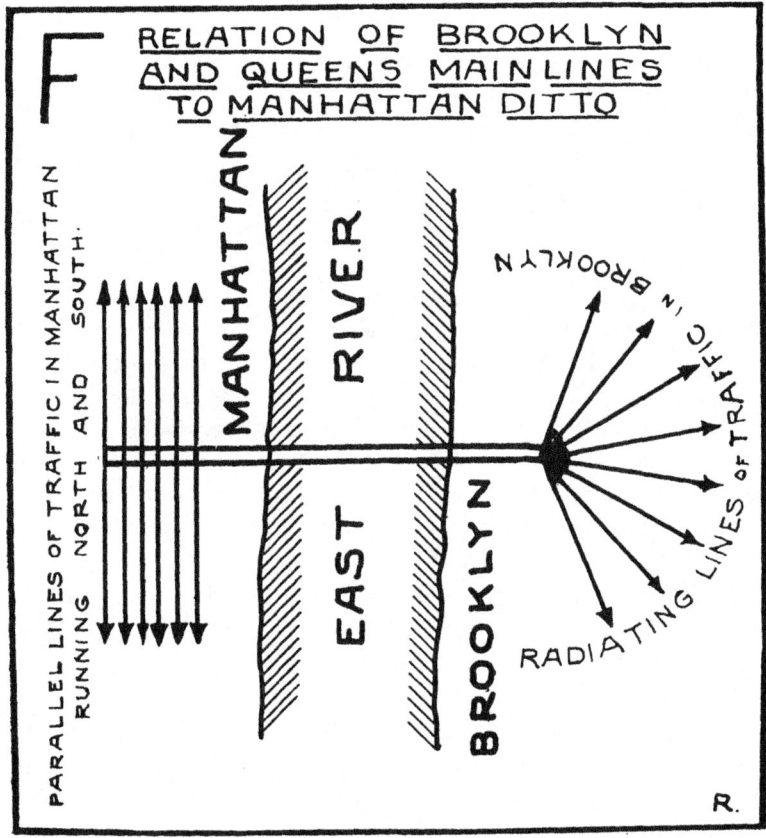

population through its own business district and across the East river to Manhattan."—W. W. Wheatly, page 241, Proceedings N. Y. Railroad Club.

Provision should be made for a system of Brooklyn subways primarily radiating from the most available point for Manhattan connection in the vicinity of the junction of Fulton street and Flatbush avenue, (a) in the direction of Fort Hamilton, ultimately to be extended by tunnel under the Narrows to the Borough of Richmond; (b) to Flatbush; (c) to East New York, and ultimately to Flushing. Such a system to be extended along the routes noted only as fast as public interest might demand (see Plates A and C). Providing satisfactory arrangements can be effected with existing or future surface lines it might not be necessary rapidly to extend the system of through subways, although we believe the inception of the work should promptly be undertaken by the City as indicative of its purpose and to facilitate prompt extension when required* and that connection with our New Jersey suburbs (see Plate A) should be planned and developed as a part of the same general system.

As now proposed by Mr. Parsons, these Brooklyn subways, like those planned by the Rapid Transit Commission for Manhattan, so tie into the existing subway systems as to make independent bidding for operation impossible unless a second river tunnel to the Battery shall be built coincidently with the proposed routes, or unless the facilities of the East river bridges be availed of. This should be done in case a satisfactory short-term lease with advantageous provisions for transfer cannot be made with the Belmont syndicate in advance.

Connections by deep subway between the Brooklyn Bridge entrance and the proposed projection of the Manhattan Bridge to Flatbush avenue should be effected (see Plate A).

We also suggest for consideration (although not here noted on the map) the future practicability of a marginal elevated railroad, to be constructed along the river front in Manhattan in connection with a possible double-deck treatment of the river streets (discussed in Bulletin No. 5 of this Society). Marginal Elevated Lines.

In addition to a city and suburban transit service, the probability in the near future of a direct projection of the cars and trains of the steam roads into the heart of the municipality over the local transit lines or through specially constructed tunnels should be borne in mind. As a consequence of the local electrification of the steam roads, the power-house will supplant the locomotive, and single coaches as well as trains will probably be distributed and assembled as readily as trolley cars are now handled. The railroad stations would then be relocated and become the assembling places for cars rather than for passengers. Steam Road Cars in the City.

---

* Similar extensions from the other bridges to be effected later (see Plate C) and a local Brooklyn line connecting the several bridge distributing points to be ultimately built.

North and West Approaches to New York. The New York Central Railroad approaches New York from the north and its tracks already lead far down into the island of Manhattan. The Pennsylvania road will approach from the west and from the east over the Long Island and the New York, New Haven and Hartford systems. Generally speaking, should not local easements be anticipated along north and south routes for the Central and along east and west routes for the Pennsylvania and other New Jersey roads. The Rapid Transit Commissioners have so far observed this distinction.

Control Trunk Lines to Boroughs. While it is apparent that the stategic points necessary to the successful operation of subway transit systems are to be found in the connections to be made between the bridge and tunnel approaches to Manhattan and the principal avenues leading to the centres of congestion there, it is also important for the municipality to develop and control trunk lines of communication between its several boroughs. These general lines of communication are indicated on the smaller map of the city appended. The city can never be properly organized—its people can never be decently housed—till its constituent parts are adequately connected with each other and with the distinctively Metropolitan District (see Plate C).

Future Traffic.

Possible Future Congestion. We would call attention to certain facts relating to the growth of population and the growth of street railway travel, indicative of conditions which are likely to confront the municipality in the near future. Unless careful provision is now promptly made, the city is likely to meet with disastrous checks to its development— the direct result of its failure to foresee and provide adequate transit facilities. In fact, New York City is now experiencing the penalty of its failure to intelligently anticipate existing conditions.

Manhattan Traffic Conditions. Mr. W. W. Wheatley, in a very interesting discussion of the transportation problem in Greater New York, published in the Proceedings of the New York Railroad Club, June, 1903, says:

" The population and traffic density in Manhattan, as will be seen, are far beyond those of any other large city. It is instructive, if not rather startling, to look back and discover that in Manhattan there have been no really great additions to the transit facilities during the past quarter of a century beyond the building of the Brooklyn Bridge and the elevated roads. With travel increasing almost 100 per cent. every ten years and no additions to the track mileage worthy of mention, there was bound to come a time when the existing lines would reach the limit of their capacity. That time has now arrived." * * * " Greater New York and the three tributary New Jersey counties of Hudson, Essex and Bergen give a total estimated population of 4,500,000, and it will be seen that the increase of population within the Metropolitan territory in ten years was 1,173,880, or at the average rate of over 100,000 per annum. Figured in another way, the increase within ten years was 38 per cent., or at the average of 3.8 per annum. Estimated on this basis, it appears that the metropolitan population in 1913 should be a little more than 6,000,000 people. While the growth of population has been remarkable, the growth of passenger traffic on local transportation lines has been still more remarkable. In each decade from 1870 to 1900 the passengers carried increased almost 100 per cent. A singular fact observed in the case of many growing cities is that for every one per cent. increase in population there is a relative increase of about three per cent. in the passengers carried. It is facts like these which indicate the tremendous probable increase of passenger traffic which the transportation lines of New York, and especially of Manhattan, will be called upon to handle within the next decade."

In the matter of Rapid Transit the most important considerations for the City are, first: The maintenance of effective and continuous control over new lines, and second, the acquisition of liberal provisions for transfer over these and other lines. Primary Needs of the City

The most important considerations for the public service corporations are: First, continuity of franchise grants which under a more intelligent public sentiment than has heretofore obtained can be expected only as a consequence of the assumption of greater responsibilities by the corporations and the admission by Primary Needs of Transportation Companies.

them of an increasing degree of municipal control. In this connection especial attention is directed to the practical workings of the Massachusetts law, which while it ostensibly makes the public service corporations tenants at will, has in effect the opposite result, and tends to create a sense of permanency in the continuation of the franchises (page 11). Second, the availability of the City's credit for the construction of needed additional transit facilities, private capital being in our judgment not available to meet the rapidly expanding needs of the community under the more exacting conditions of short term franchises which the City is likely to grant hereafter.

<small>Co-operation or Revocation.</small>
Existing transportation corporations must co-operate in the public interest toward systematizing and extending the municipal transit system, or, failing to do so, risk the continuance of their privileges in the streets. The late Abram S. Hewitt's prevision in this connection is here deserving of attention:

" I am aware that companies holding public grants "claim to have vested rights, but *there are no such* "*things as vested rights which can interfere with the* "*power of the community to do those things which are* "*essential for its growth, its safety and its progress in* "*civilization*. Improvident grants have been made; but, "when they come in contact with the superior rights of "the people, indemnity may be claimed and awarded, "but their existence cannot be pleaded as a bar to im-"provement. This proposition is true not only of those "companies which have their works under the streets, "but of all companies which occupy them for any pur-"pose whatever. The only theory upon which the "rights of private corporations to use the public streets "has ever been adjusted, is that they give greater facil-"ities to the purpose for which the streets were "created.

" But *the right of the City to require streets to be* "*used in such manner as will, from time to time, pro-* "*mote the general convenience of the community, is*

"*unquestionable.* A rail that would be a suitable one
"to-day may be unsuitable to-morrow, and experience
"may develop a better means of transportation through
"the streets, and the rights which private parties may
"have acquired cannot be urged as a bar to the exercise
"of the inherent and superior rights of the people. *To*
"*take an extreme case, several of the leading avenues of*
"*the city are occupied by elevated railway structures. They*
"*are found to be indispensable at this time for the wants of*
"*the public. If, at some future time, a better means of*
"*transportation should be found, there can be no doubt that*
"*these companies could be required to adopt it, or if it*
"*should become necessary, they could be compelled to re-*
"*move their structures from the streets altogether.* The
"question of indemnity and compensation would be one
"for the courts to settle; but there can be no doubt what-
"ever that, if in the course of progress and of invention the
"community should require a better means of transport
"than devised, it would be justified and have the un-
"doubted power to make the changes thus required.
"*Salus populi suprema lex.—Message of Hon. Abram S.*
"*Hewitt, Mayor, to the Board of Aldermen,* 1888.

Of the opposite theory—that the franchise corporations have Example of Opposite Theory. vested rights in the needs of New York's citizens, which they propose to insist upon as against any attempt to secure other service than their own—no better statement could be made than that of the Metropolitan (New York City) Railway Company of the issue in which it asks the Rapid Transit Commission to aid it against an alleged rival, here quoted from the *World* of October 14, 1904:

MR. VREELAND OBJECTS TO FRANCHISES FOR MCADOO ENTERPRISES.

A contest has been begun by the Metropolitan Street Railway to prevent the McAdoo Hudson river tunnel syndicate from building a subway from the foot of Christopher street to connect its tunnels with the proposed Pennsylvania terminal. President H. H. Vreeland, who makes the protest, asks for a chance to be heard before the Rapid Transit Commission. His request was granted. The McAdoo syndicate has applied for two franchises, one for a subway joining the New York entrances of the tunnels and proceeding thence to and along under West Tenth street and Sixth avenue to the Pennsylvania terminal, the other for a subway directly under West Ninth street to Third or Fourth avenue.

President Vreeland protests that the proposed McAdoo tunnels will divert from the Metropolitan Street Railway traffic which "properly belongs to them." The McAdoo chief engineer claims the traffic from New Jersey through the two tunnels would amount to 50,000,000 persons a year.

Maintenance of Control.

If the interests of the City are not betrayed by its trustees it will continue to hold the position of vantage which it now occupies in bargaining for new facilities and for the improvement of old ones. If, however, new franchises are granted as mere extensions of existing franchises and are given without considering their relation to the entire question of transportation and its control, the City will soon lose the unique power of control which it now enjoys.

The Physical City.

IS NOT THE ESSENTIAL OF A CITY'S PLAN ITS SYSTEM OF HIGHWAYS, ABOUT WHICH PEOPLE LIVE AND THROUGH WHICH THEY COMMUNICATE WITH EACH OTHER, AND SHOULD NOT PASSAGE THROUGH THESE BE MADE AS FREE AND CONVENIENT AS POSSIBLE, WHETHER ON FOOT OR BY PRIVATE OR PUBLIC VEHICLE?

City Plan Committee, Municipal Art Society,

NOVEMBER, 1904.

CALVIN TOMKINS, *Chairman.*

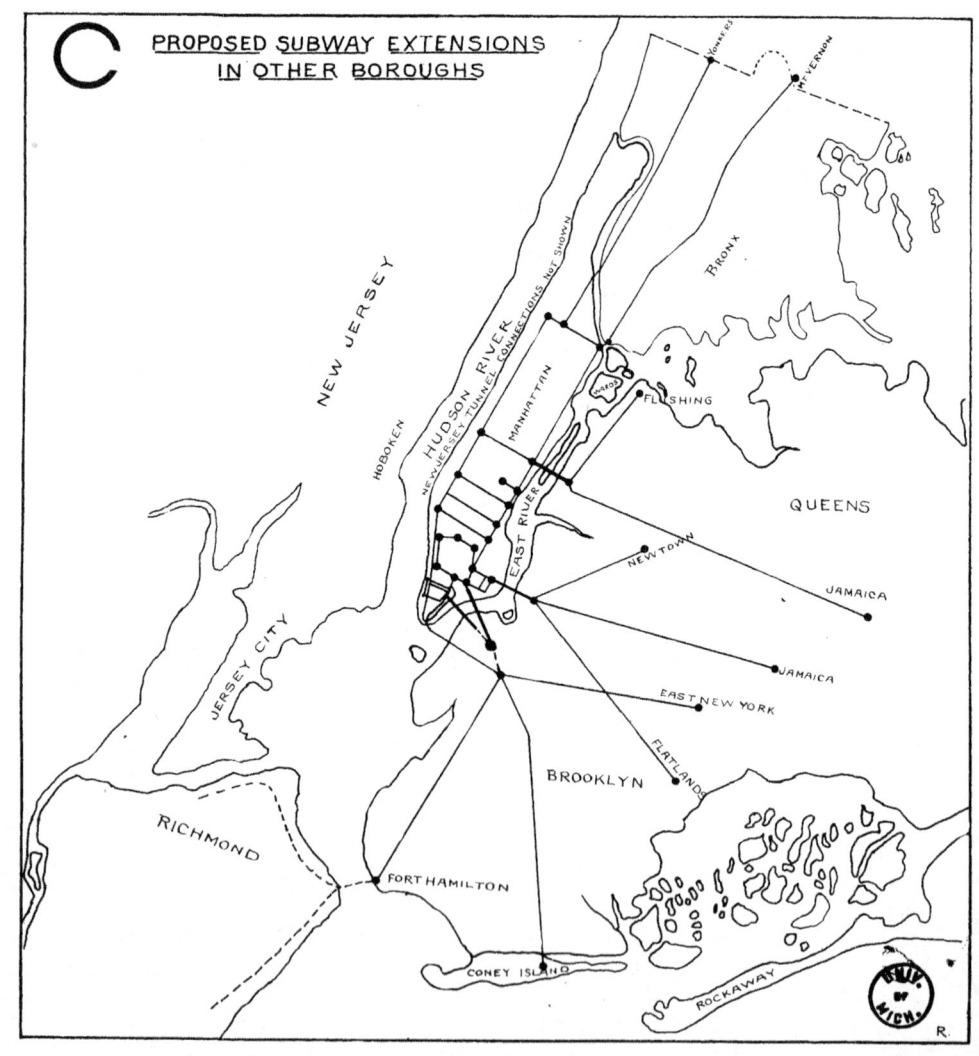

Oversized Foldout

TABLE OF CONTENTS.

	Pages.
Introduction	1
Design Should Precede Decoration	2
Criticism and Improvement	2
Causes of City Growth	3
Difficulties and Mistakes	3–6
Principles Stated by Rapid Transit Commission	6–7
Failure to Observe Same	7–10

Principles Governing Rapid Transit—
City Control	10–12
Combination	12–13
Independent Lines	14
Elevated Structures	14
Shallow and Deep Tunnels	15
Transfers	15

Bridges and Tunnels—
Control by City	15
Lateral Development of City	15
Williamsburgh Bridge Lease	16–19
Bridges as Highways	20
Collecting and Distributing Traffic	20–22
No Bridge Terminals	22
Bridge Crush and Remedy	23
Bridge Connecting Railways not Needed	24–25
Crosstown Bridge Loops	26–29
Brooklyn Radiating Subways	29

A Comprehensive Plan—
Urgency for	30
Paris Transit Plan	31
Sixth Avenue Lines	31–32
New Jersey and Long Island Routes	32–33
Letter to Rapid Transit Commission Re Routes	34–36
Independent and Dependent Systems	36
Rapid Transit Commission Plans	36–38
Municipal Art Society Plans	38–42

Future Traffic	42–43
Primary Needs of City	43
Primary Needs of Transit Companies	43–44
Co-operation or Revocation	44
Statement, Abram S. Hewitt	44–45
The Physical City	46

Bulletins of the Municipal Art Society may be secured by addressing the Secretary, No. 37 West Thirty-fourth street, either in sets or by single number.

The list of bulletins for the season 1903-'04 is appended.

Bulletin No. 1.—REPORT OF COMMITTEE ON STREET SIGNS, ISLES OF SAFETY, AND REARRANGEMENT OF COLUMBUS CIRCLE.

Bulletin No. 2.—REPORT OF CITY PLAN COMMITTEE, ON CITY HALL SQUARE AND BOOKLYN BRIDGE TERMINALS.

Bulletin No. 3.—REPORT OF CITY PLAN COMMITTEE, ON THE PASSENGER TRANSPORTATION SYSTEM OF NEW YORK. Calvin Tomkins, Chairman, 1903.

Bulletin No. 4.—REPORT OF CIVIC CENTRES COMMITTEE. J. G. Phelps Stokes, Chairman.

Bulletin No. 5.—REPORT OF COMMITTEE ON THOROUGHFARES. Charles R. Lamb, Chairman.

Bulletin No. 6.—REPORT OF CITY PLAN COMMITTEE, ON MANHATTAN BRIDGE CONNECTIONS.

Bulletin No. 7.—REPORT OF COMMITTEE ON DECORATION OF PUBLIC BUILDINGS. A. D. F. Hamlin, Chairman.

Bulletin No. 8.—REPORT OF COMMITTEE ON DECORATION OF PUBLIC SCHOOLS. George E. Bissell, Chairman.

Bulletin No. 9.—REPORT OF COMMITTEE ON PARKS. Henry Woodward Sackett, Chairman.

Bulletin No. 10.—EXTRACTS FROM REPORT TO THE BOARD OF ESTIMATE AND APPORTIONMENT, by Nelson B. Lewis, Engineer-in-Chief.

Bulletin No. 11.—PIPE GALLERIES FOR NEW YORK. James C. Bayles, Ph. D.

Bulletin No. 12.—REPORT OF COMMITTEE ON FLOWERS, VINES AND AREA PLANTING. Mrs. Edward Hegeman Hall, Chairman.

Bulletin No. 13.—DISCUSSION OF MANHATTAN BRIDGE PLANS, CITY PLAN COMMITTEE. Calvin Tomkins, Chairman.

Bulletin No. 14.—RAPID TRANSIT IN NEW YORK CITY, by City Plan Committee. Calvin Tomkins, Chairman, 1904.

The Municipal Art Society
of
New York.
37 West 34th Street.

BULLETIN No. 11.

PIPE GALLERIES FOR NEW YORK.

JAMES C. BAYLES, M. E., PH. D.

In the discussion of the problems of municipal art and civic refinement, the fact should not be lost sight of that until conditions which involve constant disorder and disturbance, which destroy pavements, obstruct our highways, jeopardize life and property and impede intercommunication are corrected, New York cannot be made a beautiful city, nor one of which the citizen may feel proud without a disquieting mental reservation; the "City Beautiful" will be an intangible and receding vision, and efforts to ornament and adorn will be as futile as would those directed to the architectural refinement of the city dumping boards or the conversion of the incomplete ash and garbage fills of Riker's Island into rose gardens. These rather coarse comparisons may perhaps better express my meaning than could be done in the language of euphuism.

The underground engineering of New York presents problems which demand radical and comprehensive remedy. They can be dealt with in no other way. In this sense the term underground engineering is a courtesy designation, since very little of engineering judgment and still less of engineering forethought have entered into the piping of the city for gas and water distribution and like purposes. To meet the conditions of his employment, the man entrusted with responsibility for work of this character needs to be an opportunist. The stratum under the pavement available for the accommodation of mains is so crowded in many parts of New York with old mains and new, live mains and dead, electric ducts, sewers, drains and the like, that to find room for another or to maintain those now in place involves the exercise of great ingenuity and recourse to expedients which would be inexcusable if they were not unavoidable. To solve the problems thus presented is to engineering as the guessing of conundrums is to exact mathematics.

Street Excavations.

It should require no argument to show that New York cannot be a clean, orderly or beautiful city, nor one comfortable and safe for occupation, until street excavation is minimized. Undertakings like the Rapid Transit Subway, the Pennsylvania terminal and its interborough tunnel, the New York Central terminal, etc., belong in a classification by themselves. Great and permanent public improvements necessarily involve present sacrifices for the attainment of future benefits. All that the citizen has the right to ask is that when begun they shall be finished as quickly as possible and with the least practicable inconvenience of traffic and travel. To work which has to be done over and over again, each time with the destruction of costly pavements and the creation of a serious and cumulative public nuisance, it is proper that emphatic objection be offered by every one in whose bosom a spark of civic pride remains alive.

The statistics of street excavation for one purpose or another connected with the laying, replacement, tapping and maintenance of underground conduits, give startling totals. Those for the Borough of Manhattan I have compiled for one year, as follows:

The number of street openings for which no permits were required for the Borough of Manhattan, in 1902, was 3,941.

Of these, 2,919 were for access to water mains and 1,022 for access to sewers. The longitudinal street trenching during 1902 was as follows:

For laying electric main conductors............ 50.38 miles
For new gas mains............................. 2.42 miles
For steam mains............................... 142 feet
For salt water mains.......................... 111 feet
For the overhauling of mains.................. 40.97 miles
For electrical long services.................. 5.81 miles

Total, 99 miles; 3,318 feet.

The street openings for subsidiary connections and repairs were:

For gas....................................... 14,468
For electrical................................ 5,467
For steam..................................... 624
For other purposes............................ 6

Total 20,565

An analysis of street openings for service connections and repairs makes the following showing of distribution:

COMPANY.	SERVICES.	REPAIRS.	TOTAL.
For Electricity—			
Consolidated Tel. & Elec. Subway Co..	1,159	316	1,475
Empire City Subway Co., Ltd..........	1,792	751	2,543
N. Y. Telephone Co.		3	3
Commercial Construction Co...........		1	1
Western Union Telegraph Co		3	3
N. Y. Fire Department................	2	1	3
United Elec. Light and Power Co	3		3
N. Y. Edison Co......................		1	1
Total...................	2,956	1,076	4,032

COMPANY.	SERVICES.	REPAIRS.	TOTAL.
For Gas— Consolidated Gas Co............	865	5,159	6,024
For Steam— N. Y. Steam Co............	55	347	402
For Salt Water Pipes— G. B. Seely's Son............		2	2
For Refrigeration— Manhattan Refrigerating Co......	2		2
Total............	3,878	6,584	10,462

In addition there were 157 emergency openings made without permit during the hours when the office of the Commissioner of Public works was closed. They were for the purpose of dealing with dangers which could not be neglected even long enough to obtain official authority for stopping them:

N. Y. Edison Co...................................... 46
Consolidated Gas Co.................................. 110
Empire City Subway Co., Ltd......................... 1

Total 157

The figures for 1903 are somewhat larger, but not different enough to warrant giving in detail. The year 1902 was typical.

The condition of the streets of New York has been a scandal and a reproach for years, and especially since the cobblestones and Belgium blocks of the earlier period of municipal development gave place, first to wood and then to the asphalt—the form of pavement which least accommodates itself to the constant excavation necessary to give access to subterranean pipes, ducts, sewers, house drains, service pipes and wires. No sooner is a street made smooth and beautiful with this elastic and tenacious surface than the necessity arises for piercing it here and there, and often trenching it longitudinally and transversely, until it is seamed and scarred in every direction. Bad as are the conditions due to this constant street excavation, those which would arise from the refusal of the municipal authorities to allow it would be incomparably worse. Neglected gas and water leakage, the congestion of sewers, street and house explosions and the restriction of electrical communication, would make New York uninhabitable, not merely in a figurative sense, but literally. The average citizen sees but one side of this question. He knows little of what is going on under ground, but is profoundly concerned with the constant street obstructions from which he suffers, deplores the apparent unthrift of the municipal administration in providing excellent and costly pavements only to permit them to be quickly and utterly destroyed, and is incensed at the apparent negligence which characterizes the action of those who should hasten to repair the ruthless damage thus inflicted upon the most valuable of public assets—our streets and avenues.

The Vicissitudes of a Pavement.

As a little wholesome humor is never out of place, I am tempted at this point to quote some verses written by a Chicago "poet," which have at least the interest of showing that we are not alone in our troubles with asphalt:

> They took a little gravel,
>   And they took a little tar,
> With various ingredients
>   Imported from afar.
> They hammered it and rolled it,
>   And when they went away
> They said they had a pavement
>   That would last for many a day.
>
> But they came with picks and smote it
>   To lay a water main;
> And then they called the workmen
>   To put it back again.
> To run a railway cable
>   They took it up some more;
> And then they put it back again
>   Just where it was before.

O, the pavement's full of furrows;
There are patches everywhere;
You'd like to ride upon it,
But it's seldom that you dare.
It's a very handsome pavement;
A credit to the town;
They're always diggin' of it up
Or puttin' of it down.

It would indicate a very crude and imperfect comprehension of the exigencies of gas and water distribution to assume that any of the street excavation, of which our citizens so justly complain, is done for any other reason than that it is unavoidable in the circumstances. Such excavation is costly, especially as it involves the expense of repavement. In a report on this subject made by me in November, 1903, to the Commissioner of Public Works, this subject is discussed very frankly and truthfully as follows:

No more unjust criticism can be directed against the Department of Public Works than that which relates to the granting of permits for street excavations. Let any one who reasons on such subjects imagine what would be the consequences, as affecting the industrial, commercial and social life of the city, if the Department of Public Works had power to conserve the pavements by refusing such permits, the disposition to exercise this power arbitrarily and unconditionally and the ability to sustain its position of obstinate opposition to other improvements than those insuring good street surfaces. Franchise privileges would be nullified; citizens would be deprived of conveniences and advantages which have come to be regarded as necessities of urban life; and in districts already piped and provided with electric conductors underground conditions would quickly be established which would render them uninhabitable. I learn on good technical authority that the underground leakage of illuminating gas in Manhattan at present exceeds three millions of cubic feet per annum. Whether it is more or less, it is certainly enormously great, and gives rise to conditions which involve the gravest dangers to life and property. If the constant repairs which are now made and which involve the constant cutting of pavements and the obstruction of streets by holes and trenches were required to be remitted even for one year, the present leakage might, and probably would, become intolerable. Neither persons nor property would anywhere be safe. If the accidents occurring in electric ducts could not be dealt with promptly and thoroughly, great investments in underground distribution would be destroyed and consumers depending upon currents for light and power purposes, and for communication, as well as such systems of signaling as the fire alarm and police services, would be destroyed. If the water mains and services could not be looked after and kept in such repair as is possible, the underground waste, at present perhaps a third of the daily supply, would quickly increase to such a volume that consumption would be curtailed and the supply available for fire protection would not at any time or anywhere be sufficient to prevent sweeping and disastrous conflagration. These are a few of the many evils which would follow an effort to protect the pavements of Manhattan by refusing permission to cut and destroy them to those who maintain underground distribution of gas, water and electricity. No permits for new constructive work are granted between about December 15 and March 1, for the reason that damages to pavements cannot be repaired in cold weather. But neither then nor at any other time can permits for the thousands of emergency repairs necessary to be made be long withheld nor finally refused. Relief from conditions which the public would quickly deem intolerable would be found in mandamus proceedings against the head of this department, and the courts would take very peremptory action. The solution of this phase of the municipal problem is found in the plan of pipe galleries, which must sooner or later be built under every important street and avenue of New York.

It will be conceded by the Commissioner of Public Works and by every officer of his department, as freely as the most enthusiastic reformer of municipal abuses could wish, that the cutting and carving of pavements laid at great cost, to do what it would seem at first glance should have been done before they were laid, is deplorable from every point of view and that it involves a distressing waste of municipal property, besides entailing incalculable public damage and discomfort. If, however, it is considered what would happen if such excavation for repairs were forbidden, it will be seen that still greater evils would result, even if the power to forbid them resided with this department; but it is impossible to anticipate what will occur to subsurface structures and provide against their getting out of order for any definite length of time. However, the department does the best it can in the circumstances to have these structures in good condition at the time the street is first asphalted. To secure this, as soon as a contract is let for the asphalting of a street all corporations are notified that they must proceed immediately to overhaul all subsurface structures which they may own and place them in good condition prior to the work of asphalting the street being commenced; and, in addition to this, they are notified that no permits will be issued by this department to open the street after it has been finally asphalted, for the period of one year, except in cases of great emergency.

Unfortunately, this emergency arises in most instances very much under a year—sometimes, indeed, as soon as the pavement is laid.

From the point of view of the Department of Water, Gas and Electricity, and even more so from that of private corporations owning mains and conduits, street excavations are in the highest degree burdensome. Their cost would pay satisfactory interest on a very large increase of corporate capitalization, and with the expenses of main maintenance, leakage losses and damage claims minimized, gas franchises and probably electric franchises would enormously increase in value. Without important main leakage New York would have in its present sources of supply in the Croton Valley water enough for the use and waste of certainly twice its present population.

Under the conditions now existing, and which will continue to exist as long as mains and conduits are buried in the ground, such condemnation of our city pavements as was made by the Grand Jury in its presentment of July 28, 1903, is a waste of time and paper. What, for example, is the use of thus cataloguing the obvious evils of holes in asphalt pavements?

BUSINESS—Delay and interference with transportation, expensive wear and tear of trucks, unnecessary damage to limb, and consequently to life, on the part of the truck horses, with resultant uncalled-for loss to their owners.

SANITATION—The sprinkling of the streets, properly at its maximum at this season of the year, causes an accumulation of water and street refuse matter in these cavities, which necessarily resolve themselves into offensive and objectionable conditions to which the public should not be exposed.

STREET CLEANING—Prompt and proper sweeping and cleaning of the streets is an important municipal function, at all seasons of the year; but in summer time, decomposition of street refuse is a distinct menace to public health, which is augmented by the existence of holes and breaks in the asphalt pavements. Many yards of pavement in good condition can be properly cleaned while a representative of the Street Cleaning Department is consuming time by excavating accumulated matter from the holes which should not exist.

ORDINARY TRAVEL—Aside from the demands of business in transportation of merchandise, and aside from the question of public health, nearly every character of locomotion (other than that of the street railways) is interfered with and rendered uncomfortable and destructive of valuable time and property when the pavements are not in proper order.

We know all this very well. The question of practical interest is: How can these conditions be corrected? The answer is: They cannot, so long as our pavements are laid over a tangle of decaying and disintegrating pipe lines, to which in the one Borough of Manhattan alone access must be had by a hundred miles of longitudinal trench and more than twenty thousand pits and cross-cuts annually. A trench, a pit or a cross-cut cannot be back filled so solidly nor repairing done so perfectly, that it does not locally ruin the pavement in which it is made.

Pipe Galleries Abroad.

The pipe gallery is no experiment. In the mass of exact information I have been able to gather concerning the results attending the building and operation of such structures in Europe, no one fact interests me more than that recorded by Mr. A. Brown, Borough Engineer of Nottingham, England. One of the main thoroughfares of that city is Victoria street. On it stands the General Post Office and many of the principal business buildings, and it has a heavy traffic. In 1866 it was provided with a pipe gallery, in which were grouped the water and gas mains, the sewer and all the high and low tension wires of that thoroughfare. Mr. Brown has assumed professional responsibility for the statement, in a paper before a very critical audience, the British Association of Municipal and County Engineers, that in the twenty-five years following the completion of this work not a stone was lifted from the pavement of Victoria street, and during that time not a penny was spent on repairs of roadway.

Think of what that means! Think of what anything like it would mean to New York! If a pavement in this city remains undisturbed for twenty-five hours it is cause for congratulation; if it should stay so for twenty-five days it would "break the record."

The pipe gallery system of Nottingham was begun in 1861, and has been continued ever since. Its cost has averaged $88,000 per mile, everything included, and the interest charge to the city over and above the annual rentals collected, is 2 per cent. This shows a large enonomy in the minimized leakage of gas and water, in main maintenance and in repairs and paving costs. The results are perfectly satisfactory to the citizens.

The London pipe galleries were begun in 1861 in a new street opened between Covent Garden and St. Martin's Lane. The system has since been extended as fast and as far as opportunity offered, and is of such conspicuous public benefit that the County Council is committed to the policy of making it part of every scheme of street improvement undertaken under its direction. The details of London practice are of technical rather than popular interest. In design the pipe galleries of that city seem crude and incomplete, and an American engineer would probably hesitate to imitate them in all respects, but they serve their purpose admirably. Some months ago I had a long and instructive conversation—several, indeed—with Mr. Maurice Fitzmaurice, Chief Engineer of the London County Council, covering the whole subject of his pipe gallery experience. I asked how it was that the approval of British electricians could be had for bunching conductors together in troughs and hanging them from pendant and side-wall brackets, and was told that they had no grounds for objection, in that the method had given them no trouble. I asked what happened in the event of crosses and short circuits, and was told that these were of infrequent occurrence, and that nothing happened. I asked what provision was made for draining the galleries to dispose of water which might leak from defective joints or gush from fractured mains, and was told that all the water which ever found its way into them from any source gathered at low points and was removed in pails without inconvenience. I asked about induced ventilation to dispel gas leakage, and was told that none had been provided, for the reason that there was no gas leakage. Permits were freely issued to plumbers to take torch lamps into the tunnels when needed in making connections. I asked Mr. Fitzmaurice if I might smoke in walking through the galleries, and he assured me that there was not the least objection to my doing so, and that I might strike matches to light my cigarette as often as I needed to. The only rule against smoking applies to workmen, who are not permitted to smoke in working hours, under or above ground.

If time served an instructive comparison might be drawn between these conditions and the annual leakage of some three thousand millions of cubic feet of gas from buried mains under the relatively impervious pavements of Manhattan.

St Helens, one of the most enterprising of the North of England municipalities, has begun a system of pipe galleries, and will extend it as rapidly as possible. Mr. G. J. C. Brown, Borough Engineer, speaks of it in a very practical way as follows:

> The object of the subway is to avoid taking up the granite street with its concrete foundations for the purpose of relaying or repairing gas and water mains or electric cables. As the Corporation had to repave the streets in equipping the tram lines for electrical traction, the question was brought before the various committees as to whether it would not be more economical and satisfactory, in view of the narrowness of the streets, the number of the mains and the unsatisfactory and costly results of interfering with the surface and foundations of the streets, to construct a subway by which the whole of the works beneath could be inspected and repaired without interfering with the roadway or the traffic. The Borough, Water and Gas Engineers were sent to London and Nottingham to inspect the subways there, and it was found that in them were carried the gas, water, electric light, hydraulic supply and telegraph and telephone cables, all of which it was expected would eventually be found in the St. Helens Subway.

This states the argument for the pipe gallery in few words. The sewers of Paris, which also serve as pipe galleries, are probably too well known to need detailed description. Their utility is summed up very clearly, and with convenient brevity, by *Engineering News* in an editorial article, from which I quote as follows:

The almost perfect condition of the Paris streets is intimately connected with the fact that the disturbance of the street surfaces by pipe trenches is practically eliminated. Water and gas pipes, telegraph and telephone wires, pipes for compressed and hot air, and the entire tangle of fixtures and appliances buried under the streets of other cities, are here disposed of in roomy, well-ventilated and well-lighted subways. Aside from the fact that this disposition does away with cutting into and replacing the pavements and prevents the obstruction of the streets by poles and overhead wires, there are other economic advantages. Pipes buried in the ground are usually left to take care of themselves until some radical and apparent defect or leakage makes repairs imperative, not only on the pipes but on the streets as well. In the Paris subways the pipes are always accessible; they can be kept in thorough repair and will consequently last longer; the smallest leak is at once detected and checked, and waste is prevented. Finlly, when a new and better system is devised for any purpose, old fixtures can be removed and new ones put in with a minimum of expense as compared with methods elsewhere. In New York, under many streets, old, unused lines of gas and other pipes are rusting slowly away, interfering with street excavations and causing settlement as they collapse, simply because it will not pay to dig them up. With a subway system this would be impossible. One thing is certain: until some subway system is built we (New York) can never have good and permanent street pavements. And it is also certain that the perpetuation of present methods means, in a term of years, the waste of a sum of money equivalent to the cost of even the Paris subways; waste in the constant renewal of pavements, increased cost of street cleaning, leaking pipes and the increased money spent in laying, maintaining and changing the present network of pipes and wires under our highways.

Milan has the beginning of a pipe gallery system under its principal avenue, the Via Dante, which Dr. Albert Shaw, in his admirable work, "Municipal Government in Continental Europe," describes as follows:

The Via Dante was constructed as the direct approach from the heart of the city to the curved front of the symmetrical new park. It is paved with wooden blocks on a concrete foundation, is lighted with electricity and is traversed by an electric street railway. But it is more notable for its underground construction than for its beautifully executed surface; for, apart from the main sewers, there are subways on either side of the street, 6 feet high by 4 or 5 feet wide. These subways adjoin the front foundation walls and make it easy to inspect and repair the drain-pipes which connect the houses with the sewers. Within the subways are placed the water-pipes, gas-pipes, electric wires, etc., and passages extend from them to the main sewers. It is considered in Milan that no street elsewhere in Europe so completely embodies the best principles of construction—below the surface if not above—as the New Via Dante.

Pipe Galleries for New York.

The history of the movement to provide pipe galleries for the principal streets and avenues of New York is well calculated to discourage further effort in this direction. It has thus far been impossible to awaken any intelligent or sustained public interest in this subject, and this apathy has been taken advantage of by corporations jealous of any encroachment upon what they have come to regard as their ownership of the streets of New York and their right to dig in them as freely as one might in his own garden, to defeat legislation, deny appropriations and restrain by injunction the efforts of the Borough President to do something practical. In a very quiet and discreet way these corporations are very potent forces in defeating every movement in the direction of reform which they do not initiate, and the results of which they will not own and control. We shall never have even the beginning of a pipe gallery system in New York until it is demanded by public opinion in terms so unmistakable that it is not susceptible of misinterpretation, and so emphatic that the Mayor, Aldermen and members of the Board of Estimate and Apportionment will not deem it safe to "smiling, put the question by."

It should be regarded as a crime against the public interest that pipe galleries were not built in connection with every foot of Rapid Transit Subway thus far constructed. This was not the fault of the Rapid Transit Commission nor of its accomplished Chief Engineer, Mr. William Barclay Parsons. In the report of the Plans Committee just submitted, relative to proposed extensions of the existing system, we find the following:

It has always been the desire of the Board, and so far as legal limitations would permit it has been the policy of the Board, to provide for pipe galleries to accommodate pipes, wires, sewers and other subsurface structures. In the general plan for the rapid transit railroad now under construction, it was expressly provided that along Elm street suitable galleries might be placed at the outside of the exterior tracks, and on April 19, 1900, the Board passed a resolution requiring the contractor to construct such pipe galleries on Elm street, between the south side of Worth street and the north side of Astor place. Such construction was actually begun, and continued until about November 1, 1900, on which date a communication was received from the city authorities, stating it as the opinion of the Departments of Sewers and Water Supply that the interests of the city would be best served by not locating either the sewers or the water pipes in such galleries. It was therefore determined by the Rapid Transit Board, in deference to the views expressed, not to proceed further with such construction.

In order to enable the Board to effectually deal with the subject. legislation will be necessary, which should enable it to provide for the construction of pipe galleries in connection with and as a part of the construction of any proposed new lines wherever the Board, in its discretion, might think such pipe galleries desirable.

Your committee may add that whatever legislation on these subjects may be proposed, they consider it very expedient that separate bills should be introduced dealing with the separate subjects upon which legislation may be desired, so that if opposition should develop to any particular proposal, the defeat of such proposal would not involve the failure of legislation upon other points to which no opposition developed.

That the opposition here suggested may be expected is very clearly shown by the incidents connected with the effort to provide pipe galleries for lower Broadway, in connection with the section of subway now building from Ann street to Bowling Green. Hon. Jacob A. Cantor, President of the Borough of Manhattan, eager to identify his administration with the initiation of this important step in municipal progress, secured reports and estimates of the cost of the work to be built coincidently with the construction of the subway. Under what were assumed to be his ample powers he employed an engineer, who made the necessary plans in full detail. An appropriation of $100,000 for beginning the work was obtained from the Board of Aldermen, and the authorization of a bond issue for the amount deemed necessary for the prosecution of the work during the last quarter of 1903 was secured from the Board of Estimate and Apportionment. At this point it looked very much as if the work was assured. Specifications were prepared and printed and bids invited. On the day the bids were to be opened and the contract let, an injunction was served on the Borough President, returnable the following day on an order to show cause why it should not be made permanent, on the ground that the President of the Borough had no power to build pipe galleries under the charter. The argument was heard, and after a very leisurely consideration, during which time Persident Cantor had been succeeded in office by the newly-elected Borough President, the injunction was made permanent. And so the matter stands. For the information of those for whom it may have interest, I give herewith certain reductions from the plans made for the lower Broadway pipe gallery, for which I am indebted to the courtesy of *Engineering News*. It will be seen that the problem was approached in a very different way from that followed abroad. The plans embody all the refinements of pipe gallery engineering. High and low tension wires are effectively separated and access to them is had through separate manholes. There are no electrical conductors in the chambers devoted to gas and water mains, ventilation and drainage are provided for, and no "chances" have been taken. In the report accompanying the plans as submitted to President Cantor, the engineer of this work said:

Foreign experience in safely grouping high tension and low tension electrical conductors, gas-mains and water-mains in common chambers would seem to indicate that in designing the pipe galleries for lower Broadway excessive regard for safety has been shown in giving the electrical systems ducts in which not only are the high and low tension wires completely separated, but are wholly removed from even proximity to gas-mains. This seemed to be desirable, if not necessary, in the present instance, but I am of the opinion that in future work of like character the foreign practice hereinbefore outlined may be more closely followed with economy and safety.

It suits those opposed to the plan of pipe galleries in New York to consider them a menace to life and property. As a matter of fact the fear expressed by gas engineers in New York that the placing of their mains in subways of any kind would imperil life and property, is largely simulated. The gas engineer who cannot conduct gas in a main through a tunnel without a measurable leakage loss, or one which involves any danger even to workmen in such tunnel, should go abroad and study foreign practice. It is an interesting fact as bearing on this phase of the discussion that a considerable proportion of the gas supply of the Borough of Manhattan is now brought to it from the Borough of Brooklyn through mains laid in a tunnel under the East river. If there have been any accidents or casualties in this tunnel, or any considerable leakage of gas from the mains it carries, the facts have been carefully concealed from public knowledge. Indeed, I am told that provision for the artificial ventilation of this tunnel by means of a pipe carrying compressed air, and supplied with cocks at convenient intervals from which it might be allowed to escape and blow out inconvenient gas accumulations, has been found wholly unnecessary.

The leakage of water in distribution is an economic evil of large proportions, but it is far less serious from every point of view than the leakage of gas in distribution. It accounts for many fires and explosions. Sewers, electrical conduits, and manholes, excavations in the streets (as at Broadway and Canal street), vaults, cellars, and even business buildings and dwellings are rent and shattered by gas explosions with such frequency that a prudent man will in every case walk around a manhole cover rather than step on it. New York has had nine such explosions in one day, and through the winter season they are so frequent as almost to escape notice. Sidewalks have been blown up, many dwellings wrecked, with loss of life, and whole blocks closed to traffic by sewer eruptions. Many of our most disastrous fires are of gas origin. The only attitude of safety for the gas company is one of cordial and even eager co-operation in demonstrating that the pipe gallery is a practical remedy for what have become intolerable conditions.

JAMES C. BAYLES, M. E., PH. D.

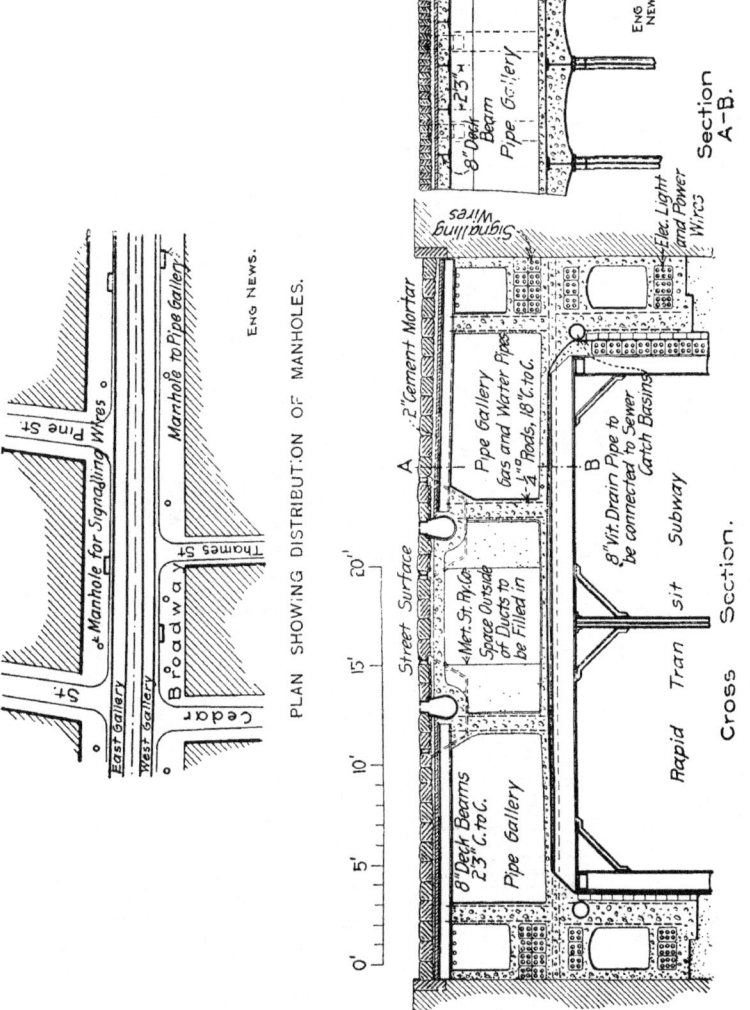

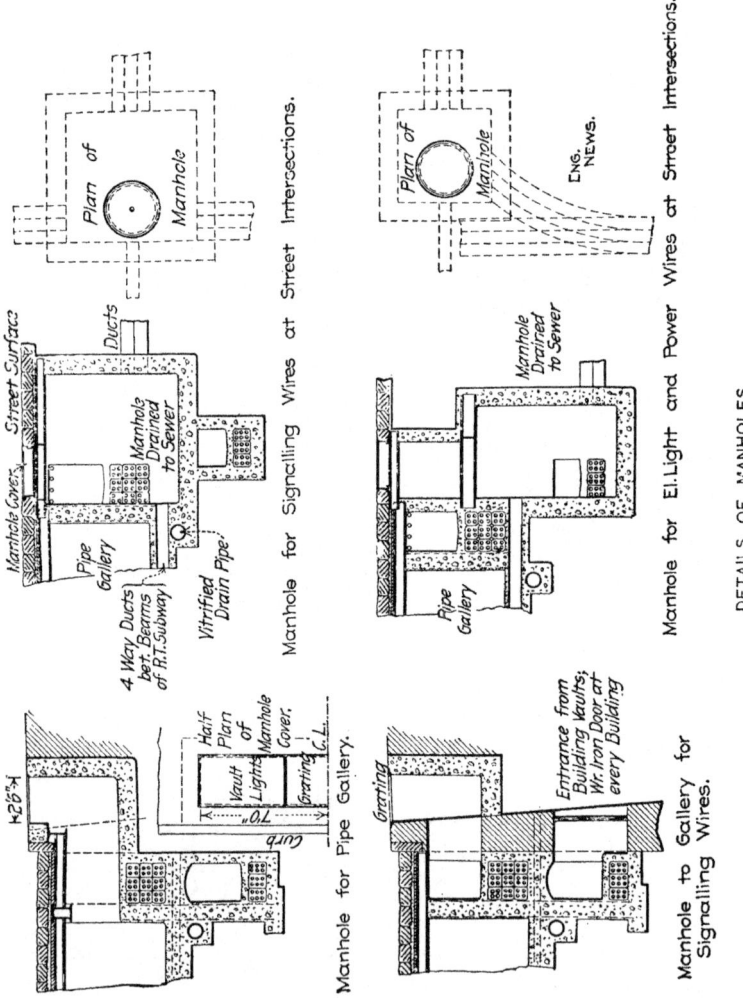

DETAILS OF MANHOLES.

OFFICERS.

President, CALVIN TOMKINS.
First Vice-President, WILLIAM T. EVANS.
Second Vice-President, JOHN J. BOYLE.
Secretary, GABRIELLE TOWNSEND STEWART.
Treasurer, EDWARD D. PAGE.
Counsel, NELSON S. SPENCER.

BOARD OF DIRECTORS.

The Mayor of New York, William T. Evans, Edward D. Page,
Karl Bitter, A. D. F. Hamlin, George B. Post,
John J. Boyle, F. Benedict Herzog, F. Wellington Ruckstuhl,
George W. Breck, Charles R. Lamb, Nelson S. Spencer,
Charles Cooper, H. A. MacNeil, J. G. Phelps Stokes,
William S. Crandall, George L. Morse, Calvin Tomkins,
John DeWitt Warner.

Bulletins of the Municipal Art Society may be secured by addressing the Secretary, No. 37 West Thirty-fourth street, either in sets or by single number. The list of bulletins for the season 1903–04 is appended.

Bulletin No. 1.—REPORT OF COMMITTEE ON STREET SIGNS, ISLES OF SAFETY, AND REARRANGEMENT OF COLUMBUS CIRCLE.

Bulletin No. 2.—REPORT OF CITY PLAN COMMITTEE, ON CITY HALL SQUARE AND BROOKLYN BRIDGE TERMINALS.

Bulletin No. 3.—REPORT OF CITY PLAN COMMITTEE, ON THE PASSENGER TRANSPORTATION SYSTEM OF NEW YORK. Calvin Tomkins, Chairman.

Bulletin No. 4.—REPORT OF CIVIC CENTRES COMMITTEE. J. G. Phelps Stokes, Chairman.

Bulletin No. 5.—REPORT OF COMMITTEE ON THOROUGHFARES. Charles R. Lamb, Chairman.

Bulletin No. 6.—REPORT OF CITY PLAN COMMITTEE, ON MANHATTAN BRIDGE CONNECTIONS.

Bulletin No. 7.—REPORT OF COMMITTEE ON DECORATION OF PUBLIC BUILDINGS. A. D. F. Hamlin, Chairman.

Bulletin No. 8.—REPORT OF COMMITTEE ON DECORATION OF PUBLIC SCHOOLS. George E. Bissell, Chairman.

Bulletin No. 9.—REPORT OF COMMITTEE ON PARKS. Henry Woodward Sackett, Chairman.

Bulletin No. 10.—EXTRACTS FROM REPORT TO THE BOARD OF ESTIMATE AND APPORTIONMENT, by Nelson B. Lewis, Engineer-in-Chief.

Bulletin No. 11.—PIPE GALLERIES FOR NEW YORK. James C. Bayles, Ph. D.

Bulletin No. 12.—REPORT OF COMMITTEE ON FLOWERS, VINES AND AREA PLANTING. Mrs. Edward Hegeman Hall, Chairman.

MEMORIAL FROM THE MUNICIPAL ART SOCIETY TO THE RAPID TRANSIT COMMISSION.

To the Rapid Transit Commission,
 ALEXANDER E. ORR, President,
 No. 320 Broadway, City:

NOVEMBER 9, 1904.

DEAR SIR—Understanding that your Commission has called a halt in the defacement of the subway, for advertising purposes. On behalf of the Municipal Art Society, I respectfully urge that while your Board take prompt action to abate the existing nuisances, it refrain from any act or expression that might be inferred to assume any jurisdiction on your part to permit advertising. Our reason for this request is that after examination of the law, by the counsel of the Society, it seems clear to us that you have no such power. As to this, your Commission has no power beyond that given it by law. The law gives you none:

"The Rapid Transit Act (sec. 6) authorizes the Board of Rapid Transit Railroad Commissioners to prepare plans and specifications for the construction of a railway including appurtenances, deemed by it necessary to secure the greatest efficiency, public convenience and safety including plans and specifications * * * for landing places, buildings, platforms stairways * * * and other suitable appliances incidental and requisite to what the said Board may approve as to the best and most efficient system of rapid transit in view of the public needs and requirements."

Private advertising is not a public need or requirement, or necessary to the efficiency of the railway or to public convenience or safety.

The Act (sec. 35) further authorizes the Board for and in behalf of the City to enter into a contract for the construction of such road "in accordance with the plans and sepcifications so adopted * * * and on such terms and conditions, not inconsistent with the aforesaid plans and specifications, as said board shall determine to be best for the public interests * * * Such contract shall also provide that, the person, firm or corporation so contracting to construct said road or roads shall * * * equip, maintain and operate said road or roads for a term of years * * * upon such terms and conditions as to the rates of fare to be charged and the character of service to be furnished and otherwise as said board shall deem to be the best suited to the public interests, and subject to such public supervision and to such conditions, regulations and requirements as may be determined upon by said board."

The contract, in brief, is to be one solely for the construction and operation of a railroad.

As to the provision in your operating contract:

"the contractor shall not permit advertisements in the stations or cars, which shall interfere with easy identification of stations or otherwise with efficient operation."

While this probably reserves to the Commission the right to exclude advertisements, even though otherwise lawfully installed, it so clearly inhibits rather than permits, that had our Society years since attacked this contract on the ground that by purporting to grant advertising privileges you had exceeded your powers, you might successfully have defended it on the ground that it did no such thing.

Again the Act provides:

(sec. 63) *that the road when constructed, shall remain the absolute property of the City and " shall be and be deemed to be a part of the public streets and highways of said city, to be used and enjoyed by the public upon the payment of such fares and tolls, and subject to such reasonable rules and regulations as may be imposed and provided for by the Board of Rapid Transit Railroad Commissioners in said city."*

I need not dwell upon how absurd on its face is any claim that you can authorize the use of "the public streets" for private advertising purposes, whether by obstruction, defacement or otherwise, or remind you that neither the City nor the State has confered upon you the authority to do so. Besides obstructing the public streets, the presence of these signs is a defacement, and their mounting a malicious injury to public property, which on the one hand your Commission can not legally permit, and on the other has expressly forbidden. For example your contract provides:

"The stations must be finished in a decorative and attractive manner, such as is consistent with and suitable to buildings of such character."

And again:

"All details of the stations must be so arranged as to facilitate cleaning and to permit if desired a thorough washing of all parts of the stations and their approaches by means of a hose."

It is self-evident that any probable use of the subway for advertising must violate both these provisions.

As the matter now stands the public has to deal with admitted trespassers on public streets and wanton defacers of public buildings. So fully do these law-breakers appreciate this that their contracts with advertisers provide, that signs are at the risk of the latter, and that such contracts shall terminate, should the contractors have no right to lease space. From careful inquiry we conclude that the subway operators have equally well protected themselves against reclamation, even should advertising be excluded. It is highly important therefore that your Commission refrain from any action that shall either excuse these trespassers or substitute yourselves in their place.

In closing, we venture to hope that it may not be necessary for our Society to go beyond this memorial.

Respectfully submitted,

CALVIN TOMKINS,
President.

Protests by individuals and associations against the presence of advertisements in the Subway streets should be addressed to the RAPID TRANSIT COMMISSION, No. 320 Broadway, and copies sent to the Municipal Art Society, No. 37 West 34th Street.

The Society will mail additional copies of this memorial to lists or to individuals on request.

Memorial from the Municipal Art Society to His Honor the Mayor.

To Hon. GEO. B. McCLELLAN,
Mayor, City of New York,
New York:

NOVEMBER 28, 1904.

DEAR SIR—In the matter of the Subway advertising, the Municipal Art Society calls your attention to the extraordinary situation into which the city is drifting. Every late development has justified the position taken by this Society.

(1) The Rapid Transit Commission has been advised by its own counsel:

"It is perfectly plain that whatever rights the Rapid Transit Company may have to use the subway stations for advertising purposes such rights are not derived from any express grant contained in the contract, but rest solely on the claim of that company that the privilege to advertise is a recognized and customary incident of the operation of a railroad of this class * * *.

"What the Board did was to limit whatever general powers the lessee of the property would have had if the contract had been entirely silent upon the subject."

In this connection, we note that in the Boston subway, the one most nearly of this class, no advertisements whatever are permitted, though the plan and finish of its stations are far less inconsistent therewith than are our beautifully decorated structures.

It seems clear that private advertising is not an incident of operation of a railroad. It is wholly unnecessary to it. Even the steam roads do not use their stations for such purpose.

(2) The status of the subway is now conceded to be that thus defined by our Rapid Transit Act:

"The road when constructed shall remain the absolute property of the city and shall be and be deemed to be a part of the public streets and highways of said city."

As to this, the act giving no privilege to lease any portion thereof, but only that the Rapid Transit Commission may contract with some person, firm or corporation to

"Equip, maintain and operate said road or roads for a term of years."

It is equally clear that the statute permits no "lease" of this public street, and that no agreement between the contractor and the Rapid Transit Commission that the operating contract shall be called a lease can alter its real nature or extend its legal effect beyond a franchise to equip, maintain and operate the railway, while still leaving the subway a public street.

(3) The contract provides:

"The stations must be finished in a decorative and attractive manner."

And also that—

"All details of the stations must be so arranged as to facilitate cleaning and to permit if desired a thorough washing of all parts of the stations and their approaches by means of a hose."

Not merely must any ambiguity in the contract be solved in accord with these provisions, but the contractor having itself built these stations (with the City's money) is now estopped to question the binding force of these provisions—each of which is so flagrantly violated by the use for advertising it now insists upon.

(4) Finally the Rapid Transit Commission has itself decided that the present practice of the operator in this regard does—

"Interfere with the easy identifications of stations and otherwise with efficient operation."

So that the advertisers have added to defacement of public buildings and obstruction of the City's highways defiance of the Commission and flagrant disobedience of its regulations.

Except that the fact is otherwise, the Society and the public would assume that the Commission is vigorously moving to vindicate its authority, that the police are arresting this destruction of City property, and that the Corporation Counsel is seeking to recover damage already done and to enjoin a like trespass in the future.

But the fact is that for nearly a month with the greatest possible publicity these breaches of order—this destruction of public property, and this violation of contract have not, to say the least, been met with any proper vigor by the Rapid Transit Commission, the police and the representatives of the City as a property owner—this even during the past ten days; when the obvious purpose of the Interborough Company has been to anticipate injunction and to entrench itself as firmly as possible in an assured position, which it could use to deprive the City of relief except after years of delay.

Meanwhile, also notwithstanding their obvious duty not to surrender in advance any ground upon which the order of the commission may be enforced or the public interest protected—from the beginning both the present Counsel of the Commission have championed the contractor's claim, while the Chairman of the Commission has lately gone further—insisting that the Commission had explicitly contracted that the operator might use the subway for advertising.

Not to do these gentlemen injustice we annex copies of their published statements (of whose character and number there can be no question). The point thus raised is not as to their good faith but rather whether it should be left to them to protect the City. We cannot believe that any business man would longer leave his equally important private interests to agents or counsel who had so far taken the part of the aggressors upon him, and so long permitted them to strengthen their position against him; nor can we assume that the City should be less prompt and vigorous in defense of public rights and city property.

The Municipal Art Society therefore respectfully urges that under your direction subway streets be kept open and free from encroachment for advertising purposes, and that suit be at once brought by the City against the Interborough and all others responsible therefor to collect damages for the injury already done to public property, and to prevent its continuance.

    Yours respectfully,

      MUNICIPAL ART SOCIETY,
        CALVIN TOMKINS,
           President.

PUBLISHED OPINIONS.

" It seems to me, however, that we are morally obligated in the matter of these signs. Why, if the people of New York are so offended with these signs it's an easy matter to unite in a petition to the City saying they would be willing to be taxed to indemnify the company for its losses."—(Alexander E. Orr.)

" There will always be advertising signs in the present subway." * * *

" I have seen a great deal printed against the use of posters in the subway stations," continued Mr. Orr, " but the writers generally ignore the fact that the contract for the operation of the present subway distinctly gives the company the right to put up as many signs as it pleases, provided the signs do not prevent the easy identification of the stations, or interfere with the operation of the road. * * *

" But it ought to be understood from the outset that we cannot make the subway company remove all the advertisements from the subway. We have no legal or moral right to do so, for not only is it explicitly written in the contract, but it was thoroughly understood orally.—(Alexander E. Orr.)

" It is the intent of the contracting parties that will determine the whole question," said Albert E. Boardman, of counsel for the Rapid Transit Commission, speaking yesterday of the validity of the contract and the ability of the Municipal Art Commission* to fight it successfully. " If the members of the Commission and the officers of the Interborough Company, between whom the operating contract was made, are put on the stand, they will be compelled to admit that in making that contract with the operating company the question of advertising privileges was considered, and that this was deemed by the operating company as one of their available sources of income that had much to do with the terms of the contract as finally agreed upon."—(Albert B. Boardman.)

"The Commission's counsel, George L. Rives, said: ' There was no doubt of the legal right of the Interborough Company to put advertising signs in the subway subject to the limitation as to obscuring or disfiguring the stations.' "

---
* ?-Society.

Municipal Art Society
of
New York.

BULLETIN No. 22

Correspondence between New York City Officials and the President of the Municipal Art Society, regarding advertising in the McAdoo Subway.

Hon. ALEXANDER E. ORR,
 President, Rapid Transit Commission,
  No. 320 Broadway, City:

DEAR SIR—After carefully reading the certificate recently issued by the Rapid Transit Commission to the New York and Jersey Railway Company, I find no prohibition or reference of any kind to advertising.

In view of the popular disapproval of the signs in the existing subway streets and their prohibition (except by later special consent of the Rapid Transit Board) in the Brooklyn extension, I take this opportunity to write you for information as to why a similar or an absolute prohibition was not included in the McAdoo contract.

I have understood that yourself and every other member of the Board are personally opposed to advertisements, and only tolerated them to any extent whatever in connection with the first subway as a hard necessity.

Am I wrong, or does the Board believe that a similar necessity exists now, after the profit in operating underground transit has been demonstrated? In any event, is it not desirable that the matter should be provided for in advance, rather than at the opening of the subway to the public, when its unexpected defacement may again be the occasion of discontent.

Yours respectfully,

CALVIN TOMKINS,

President.

BOARD OF RAPID TRANSIT RAILROAD COMMISSIONERS,
January 20, 1905.

Mr. CALVIN TOMKINS,

President, Municipal Art Society of New York,

No. 17 Battery Place, New York:

DEAR SIR—I beg leave to acknowledge receipt of your communication of the 17th of January, with respect to the franchise to the New York and Jersey Railroad Company, and the necessity for including a prohibition as to advertising.

Your views have been brought to the attention of the Rapid Transit Board.

B. L. BURROWS,

Secretary.

JANUARY 30, 1905.

Hon. EDWARD M. GROUT,

Comptroller, City of New York,

No. 280 Broadway, City:

DEAR SIR—Under date of January 18 I wrote President Alexander E. Orr, of the Rapid Transit Commission, requesting that he define the status of advertising in the proposed franchise to the New York and Jersey Railway Company. I also suggested that, at his convenience, my letter and his reply be printed concurrently. I have since received a note from Mr. Burrowes, Secretary of the Commission, acknowledging receipt of my communication (a copy of which I inclose) and stating it had been brought to the attention of the Rapid Transit Board; the only comment being the following remark, stated to have been made by yourself, as per press reports: " Apparently Mr. Tomkins does " not realize that the McAdoo tunnel is a private enterprise, not " to be built with City money; I sympathize with the work the

"Art Society is trying to do, but really its communications are "sometimes drawn so that they are positively offensive."

We are glad to note that you sympathize with our work, and you have had more than our sympathy in the good work which you have attempted to accomplish in ameliorating subway conditions. We have intended at all times, whether speaking critically or otherwise, to address City officials with the respect due their office, and we should be pleased to have you indicate, in the communication referred to, or in any other addressed by our society to the Rapid Transit Commission, in what respect "they "are so drawn as to be offensive," other than in legitimate difference of opinion, to which we do not believe you refer.

Recalling the terse and vigorous sentences contained in your letter to Hon. Andrew H. Green, May 10, 1902, criticizing the Rapid Transit status, we believe that we have so far kept well within your own view as to the courtesy proper in addressing the Commission.

We are ready to welcome criticism, however sharp, if it is specific, and to meet it if we can do so, or to defer to it if we cannot.

We cannot admit or even fully understand your contention "that the McAdoo tunnel is a private enterprise." Do you mean that, being constructed by private parties, the McAdoo subways do not become streets? Even if so, is the public less interested that they be not disfigured? Indeed, if they cannot be protected as streets by other City authorities, is it not all the more necessary that your Commission protect them, or do you refer to the fact that a part of these subways is granted in perpetuity? If so, is it not all the more important that the public be protected against misuse and defacement? Do you consider advertising here less objectionable to the public than in the Brooklyn extension, where it has been prohibited, except by express consent of the Rapid Transit Commission, you yourself having introduced the resolution which has just been enacted by the Commission, permitting the new Fulton street station " to be used solely for railroad purposes and not for the sale of merchandise or the display of advertisements"? Do you mean that you could not have regulated or prohibited advertising in the McAdoo tunnel? In view of your own and the popular disapproval of subway advertising, why was the certificate not so drawn and advertising prohibited, or limited?

I have endeavored to follow your example in making the terms of this letter direct and specific to subserve clearness and brevity, and I have ventured to address you in preference to again addressing the Commission, since, together with his Honor the Mayor and Commissioner Smith, you seem to be the only responsive members of the Board.

I shall be pleased to have your reply at your convenience.

Yours respectfully,

CALVIN TOMKINS,
President.

DEPARTMENT OF FINANCE—CITY OF NEW YORK,
January 31, 1905.

Mr. CALVIN TOMKINS,
President, Municipal Art Society of New York,
New York City:

DEAR SIR—I have your letter of the 30th inst. The franchise of the New York and Jersey Railway Company is, in respect to advertising, the ordinary and usual franchise to operate a railroad. It does not differ from the franchises of existing surface, elevated or steam railroads in The City of New York, even from the more recent and best drawn franchises, which have been passed by the Board of Estimate and Apportionment. That is, it is a franchise to a private corporation to operate a railroad, built with private capital, having from the City only a right-of-way. It says nothing as to advertising. If advertising is a necessary and proper incident of the operation of a railroad, then advertising is lawful. If it is not such an incident of railroading, then advertising is not lawful. As a public official, I see no reason why I should take a stand against advertising *per se*. I have taken stand against advertising in or on City property as such, but I do not think that such objection lies equally against all advertising on railroads of private corporations built by private capital, even though they run on, over or under the streets. I suggest that you bring this matter to a determination by proper action in court against not only the Interborough Company, which uses the City subway, but also the lines which use the surface of the streets and the elevated structures, to test the basic question of whether or not advertising is an incidental railway use, to be inferred or implied from the broad franchise to operate a railway on, under or over the public streets.

As to the tone of your communication to the Rapid Transit Commission, you must excuse me for declining a discussion. I am glad, however, to gather from your letter that it has not been intended to offend, but only to make use of terse and vigorous sentences.

EDWARD M. GROUT,
Comptroller.

FEBRUARY 3, 1905.

Hon. EDWARD M. GROUT,
Comptroller, City of New York,
New York, N. Y.:

DEAR SIR—I have your letter of the 31st ultimo, and regret that you have not answered my queries, though to me they still seem direct; I take the liberty of stating them again.

" Do you mean that, being constructed by private parties, the McAdoo subways do not become streets?"

" Even if so, is the public less interested that they be not disfigured?"

" If they cannot be protected as streets by other city authorities, is it not more necessary that your Commission protect them?"

" Do you refer to the fact that a part of these subways is granted in perpetuity? If so, is it not all the more important that the public be protected against misuse and defacement?"

" Do you consider advertising here in the McAdoo subways less objectionable to the public than on the Brooklyn extension?"

" Do you mean that you (the Commission) could not have regulated or prohibited advertising in the McAdoo tunnel?"

"Why was the ((McAdoo) certificate not so drawn, and advertising prohibited or limited?"

I infer from your reply that you do consider that the McAdoo subways will not become streets; also that the fact that a part of them are granted in perpetuity does distinguish them (whatever may be the effect of this) from the Belmont system.

I should be pleased to have you confirm or correct my impression in this regard; adding such explanation, if not answer, as may occur to you, upon the other points noted.

I also infer from your letter a suggestion (which inference I appreciate may not be well founded) to the effect that, aside from yourself and the Mayor, the other Commissioners may not feel it their duty to specially protect the city, except as especially required so to do by the law under which they act. Our Society, however, assumes that in making the Mayor and Comptroller *ex officio* members of the Commission, the Legislature intended that, as Mayor and Comptroller, they should watch over the interests of the city as a whole.

Am I right? Or do I understand that you consider the Mayor and yourself to have no right as members of the Commission to protect the city, except as specifically required by the Rapid Transit Act?

You can see the importance of this point.

In reply to your suggestion that our Society promote a taxpayer's suit, our answer is, that we understand we can do this only upon the ground that the Commissioners, including yourself and the Mayor, are wasting or injuring public property, or dealing with it without authority, etc. We are consequently reluctant to take such action, either here or in the matter of the Belmont Subway, until every opportunity shall have been afforded the regularly constituted authorities to obviate the necessity for our doing so. We respectfully submit that this is the prior duty.*

---

* Since the above was written and mailed (the same day, in fact) I have received the very satisfactory letter of his Honor, the Mayor, relative to the removal of advertising signs from the existing subway. A copy of this letter is appended.

C. T.

As we wish to include your answer before making this correspondence public, may we not beg a reply at your earliest convenience, in order that the situation may be stated as clearly as possible.

Yours respectfully,

CALVIN TOMKINS,
President.

DEPARTMENT OF FINANCE—CITY OF NEW YORK,
February 4, 1905.

Mr. CALVIN TOMKINS,
President, Municipal Art Society,
New York City:

DEAR SIR—I have yours of the 3d inst. In my letter I said all that I care to say to you on the subject, and I think, whether you do or not, that I have sufficiently answered your questions. I must, therefore, decline either to confirm or correct your impressions or inferences, or to submit to any catechising by you. I feel, however, that it is necessary to reiterate the statement already made to you, which you do not seem to have comprehended, that advertising in the McAdoo tunnels differs in no substantial point, either in fact or of law, from advertising on the elevated railroads or in the street cars, and to renew the suggestion that you attack this whole question at its foundation by raising the issue as to whether advertising is a necessary and proper incident of operating a railroad.

EDWARD M. GROUT,
Comptroller.

NEW YORK, February 8, 1905.

Hon. EDWARD M. GROUT,
Comptroller, City of New York:

I beg to acknowledge your letter of the 4th instant. The matter is important and it is desirable that the points of difference between the McAdoo and Belmont subway grants should be clearly established, so that a correct public opinion may be developed. I consequently regret that you should not have discussed the matter more fully. I understand your argument that the legal status of advertising in the McAdoo subways may be similar to that in vogue on the elevated roads and stations, but I fear you do not appreciate the point made by the Municipal Art Society, viz.: That so far as concerns the public, defacement of the McAdoo subways and stations is precisely as offensive as similar use of the Belmont subway, and that it was therefore the plain duty of the Rapid Transit Commission to have protected the public against such defacement—and all the more so if, not being considered municipal highways, other city authorities cannot protect them.

Yours respectfully,
CALVIN TOMKINS,
President.

Mayor's Letter Regarding Removal of Subway Signs.

CITY OF NEW YORK—OFFICE OF THE MAYOR,
February 3, 1905.

The Municipal Art Society,
No. 37 West Thirty-fourth Street, New York City:

GENTLEMEN—I beg to acknowledge the receipt of your communication of November 28 in regard to the advertising signs in the subway, and to say that I have not made an earlier reply thereto because I desired to await the result of the consideration of the subject by the Rapid Transit Commission, which I thought might make any action on my part unnecessary.

When, however, the Commission took a position contrary to my view of the law, I submitted the matter for advice to the Law Department, which to-day confirms my opinion that the use of the subway for advertising signs is in violation of the City's rights. I feel justified, therefore, in taking independent action, and I have accordingly requested the Borough President to notify the contractor to remove the objectionable signs, and if within a reasonable time this demand be not complied with, that he remove them himself to the corporation yard, like any other incumbrance unlawfully upon the public highway.

GEO. B. MCCLELLAN,
Mayor.

BULLETIN No. 18.

COMMITTEE ON CITY PLAN :

CALVIN TOMKINS, Chairman.
JOHN DE WITT WARNER,   J. G. PHELPS STOKES,
FREDERICK S. LAMB.   CHARLES R. LAMB,
MILO ROY MALTBIE,   HENRY W. SACKETT.

NEW YORK CITY, December 15, 1904.

To the Honorable the Rapid Transit Commission:

GENTLEMEN—With reference to proposed transit lines along Sixth avenue from Tenth street to Thirty-second street, across Eighth street, across Thirty-fourth street and along Broadway from Union square to Forty-second street, the City Plan Committee of the Municipal Art Society desires to direct attention to certain general principles, the observance of which it believes to be essential to the successful development of the future transit needs of the City.

First—It is desirable that whatever is done should be done with reference to a comprehensive plan, the desirability for which is so convincingly set forth in the reports of your honorable Board for 1902–3.

At present the City is in complete control of the underground transit situation, excepting only as modified by the subway which has been built. With the construction of each new subway this degree of control will be curtailed unless a wise prevision is exercised, which shall plan each new line so that it will avoid conflict with lines to be subsequently built. And all new lines should be so planned as to be capable of co-ordination with the rapidly developing municipal system as regards transfers, operation and control.

Assuming each street subway level requires 20 feet perpendicular space, not more than two levels will be accessible by stairs; the third level will have to be reached by elevators. It seems to us consequently axiomatic that the comparatively few north and south avenues on Manhattan should be reserved for subways just below the surface to carry the important north and south-bound traffic. Directly under these, say at a depth of 40 feet, should run the transverse subways or moving sidewalks leading to the East and Hudson rivers, with provision for future projection to Long Island and New Jersey. Any arrangement of subways which shall interfere with this plan, while it may now serve the convenience of certain localities, will surely cause far greater inconvenience hereafter. No transit franchise whatever, should in our judgment be granted for a few blocks along Sixth avenue on the 40 foot level and none on the level immediately under the surface of the street unless provision is made whereby the City can retake it promptly whenever the development of the general municipal plan shall require resumption of the grant.

The traffic on Sixth avenue along the line of the proposed grant is already so great that the desirability of a subway arcade to serve as a sidewalk on either side of the tracks may soon become apparent; and no complicating long-term grant of privileges should be permitted to intervene. This suggestion has already been noted in the Record & Guide, October 8th, 1904.

If the New York & Jersey Company and the Hudson & Manhattan Co. ultimately expect to connect their uptown systems and downtown by way of a Sixth avenue route and extend the same northward above Thirty-second street, we think their interests will be best served by frankly avowing their purpose so to do. In that event the City could consider a desirable through route.

SECOND—*Control:* In the report of your honorable commission for 1903 the recommendation for a grant to the Hudson & Manhattan Co. for a passenger subway along Dey street from Broadway to Church street is limited as follows:
" The committee, however, does not think that the city should
" be absolutely committed to this grant. The proposed fran-
" chise provides therefor, *that in case any municipal necessity*
" *shall arise,* then upon the requirement of the board or the city,
" the location under the streets of such passenger subway, shall
" be changed or if necessary such subway entirely closed or
" surrendered."

As illustrating present and future difficulties referred to, the following cut showing the situation at the intersection of Sixth avenue, Broadway and Thirty-fourth street, is submitted.

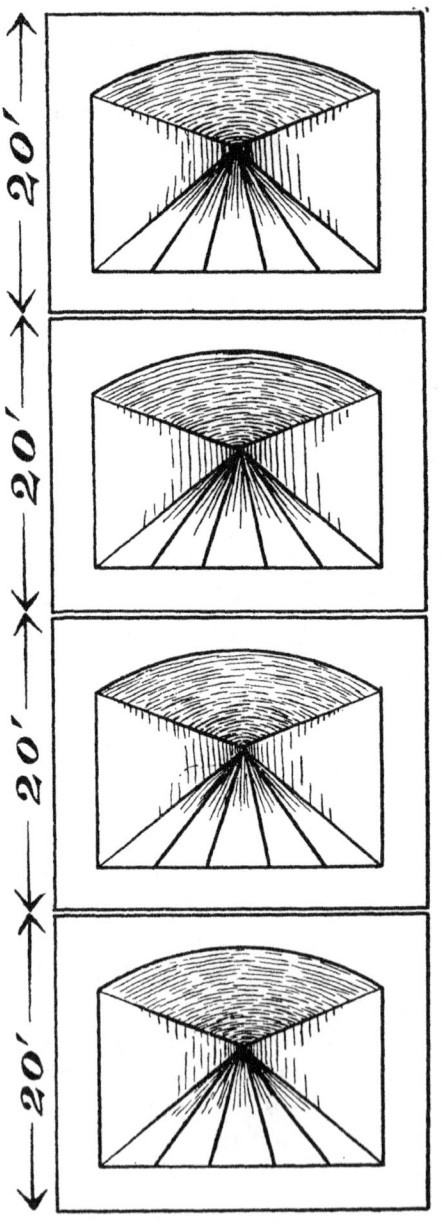

20 ft. Subway level along Sixth Avenue.

40 ft. Subway level along 34th Street.

60 ft. Tunnel level Pennsylvania Railroad along 32d St.–33d St.

80 ft. Subway level Broadway Express Service.

We believe some such wise provision, coupled with a reasonable indemnity provision should be made a part of all future franchises; and that these in themselves should be limited to periods not in excess of 25 years. Only by keeping constant control over its future subways can the City hope ultimately to obtain cheap and adequate transportation for its people.

The extension of the New York & Jersey Tunnel through Eighth street and provision for a moving sidewalk through Thirty-fourth street we believe to be highly desirable—if planned with reference to a comprehensive system, and maintained under municipal control as above noted. Moreover, by continuing these New Jersey tunnels to the East river direct connection could be made with every north and south line that serves Manhattan and The Bronx, and the enterprise thus made of most general benefit to these boroughs, as well as capable of extension under the East river and to the eastern boundary of Queens, whenever trunk cross City lines shall be needed in addition to those that can be accommodated by the bridges now planned.

Broadway traverses the City diagonally from Union square north, crossing Fifth, Sixth, Seventh, Eighth, Ninth and Tenth avenues and continuing along the line of Eleventh avenue. It is evident therefore that any subway along it, unless placed below the twenty and forty foot levels, will in the future necessitate grade crossings with the subways along the avenues or with east and west transverse subways at the above noted intersections.

On the completion of Blackwell's Island bridge, a subway across Fifty-ninth street will be absolutely necessary, as traffic on that street is already greater than the street can carry. This in turn will necessitate that the future subway tracks running along Eighth avenue be depressed to the 60-foot level at the intersection of Eighth avenue and Fifty-ninth street—as a consequence of the existing subway and the prospective transverse subway. Similar conditions hold true, but are less apparent (since the congestion is less), at the intersections of Broadway and Sixty-sixth street and Seventy-second street, with Ninth and Tenth avenues respectively.

At Forty-second street and Seventh avenue a Seventh avenue subway *can* be constructed on the 40-foot level 'provided Broadway is left clear at this level.

At the intersection of Broadway, Sixth avenue and Thirty-fourth street if a superficial tunnel shall be constructed along Broadway the transverse tunnel will run under it, on the 40-foot level. The existing Pennsylvania tunnels through Thirty-second and Thirty-third streets now occupy the 60-foot level, so that a Sixth avenue tunnel would have to be depressed to the 80-foot level—or preferably, the Broadway subway should go to that level.

A superficial tunnel along Broadway at Twenty-third street will produce complications for a Fifth avenue subway line similar to those now to be encountered at the Fifty-ninth street intersection.

It is of course presumed that these matters have received attention by your honorable body and its engineers: Inasmuch therefore as grade crossings are undesirable, unsafe and prohibitive of speed, it appears to us that Broadway above Fourteenth street, except as so far occupied by the present subway, is only available for deep tunnel express service.* If utilized for additional superficial tunnel service, it will prevent the proper utilization of Fifth, Sixth and Seventh avenues for subways.

In conclusion we again enter our plea for submission by the commission of the comprehensive plan recommended by it to its engineers in its reports for 1902–3, in contrast to a piecemeal decision, as each applicant comes forward for a franchise—and for a policy of continuous municipal control—and finally for a reasonable interval for public discussion between the publication of your plans and their final adoption by your honorable body.

Respectfully submitted,

MUNICIPAL ART SOCIETY CITY PLAN COMMITTEE,

CALVIN TOMKINS,

Chairman.

---

* A series of separate superficial subway links, equipped with moving sidewalks extending along Broadway, from Fourteenth to Twenty-third street; from Twenty-third to Thirty-fourth street; from Thirty-fourth to Forty-second street, etc., might prove very desirable for local service.

Municipal Art Society.

BULLETIN No. 19.

COMMITTEE ON CITY PLAN :

CALVIN TOMKINS, Chairman.
JOHN DE WITT WARNER, J. G. PHELPS STOKES,
FREDERICK S. LAMB, CHARLES R. LAMB,
MILO ROY MALTBIE, HENRY W. SACKETT.

NEW YORK, December 21, 1904.

To the Honorable the Rapid Transit Commission,

No. 320 Broadway, N. Y.

GENTLEMEN—Your honorable body having instructed counsel to prepare a form of contract to be entered into between the City and the New York & Jersey Railway Company, presumably on the lines of the report of your Contract Committee, made December 15, 1904, which report recommends the grant of a perpetual subway franchise across the city by way of Ninth street, as far as Second avenue,—we venture to question the desirability of such a grant, which if made, we believe will be against the interests of the City and will seriously interfere with the development of its ultimate plan of transit.

What is a grant in perpetuity? A grant for say 999 years is at least intelligible, but we believe it in order that the parties seeking such a concession, and that your honorable body, before granting such a request clearly define the term "in perpetuity." Criticism has been directed against the action of the Commission for the 75-year term of the existing municipal subway franchise. The City Charter limits franchises to 25 years. The Commission have the power to exceed this limitation, but such power carries a corresponding moral responsibility. You have refused the request of this corporation for a similar grant along Sixth avenue. Should the

City now part forever with its rights in a cross-town street that will soon be required not merely to serve New Jersey needs, but those of our own Borough of Brooklyn as well? Bridge Commissioner Best in a recent report refers to the present desirability of running the Eighth street surface cars over the Williamsburg bridge and the question of Brooklyn subway connections by bridge and tunnel through Ninth street must soon arise. If this grant shall now be made in perpetuity the city must then defer to the New York & Jersey Company. No Brooklyn cross-town connections through Ninth street can consequently be arranged except by agreement with the corporation holding a perpetual franchise in that important street. A most unjust, complicated and expensive situation will then have arisen. It would seem but ordinary prudence now to anticipate and forestall any such a contingency.

Again, Ninth street crosses all the principal north and south lines of transit of Manhattan. It will be unfortunate if the City shall not reserve some control over transfers.— Most unfortunate of all, no one can predict the engineering complications likely to arise when the City shall need the use of its north and south avenues for new subway routes.

As an example of the probable difficulties to be encountered from lack of city control, we quote from Commissioner, Comptroller Grout's statement of December 14th, as illustrating this particular matter:

" " The extension of the Hudson River Tunnel from Jersey across Manhattan will distribute people over the widest area and prevent congestion. If it were not for City Hall Park and *the present subway*, this same idea of an extended terminal would probably be carried out in connection with the Brooklyn Bridge, carrying bridge passengers as far west as Ninth avenue. This idea as far as practicable, no doubt will be carried out in planning terminals for future tunnels and bridges." "

The only impediment to the projection of a Brooklyn Bridge distributing subway directly west, under City Hall Park is to be found in the action of the Rapid Transit Commission in placing the existing station directly in front of the underground entrance to the bridge and at a level which precludes such construction.

If it is possible that this mistake should have become apparent between the inception of plans and before their completion, what similar mistakes in planning and in operation may be expected under a perpetual franchise:—Such a franchise in effect will have a dual value ;

FIRST—For obstruction, most serious to the City and most valuable to the grantee, and

SECOND in importance—for transit.

We believe it is desirable that the City should reserve continuous control over franchises to be granted. This can be equitably accomplished under the terms you have imposed upon the Sixth avenue grant, coupled with the City's right to recover the grant, say within a period of five years on payment of not to exceed double the cost of construction ; after five years the basis for recovery to be on a sliding scale of value diminishing each year, to actual value at the expiration of the twenty-fifth year period. In addition to such compensation, transit corporations will always have the aid of the citizens they serve. In case municipal exigencies shall require rearrangement of franchise, these citizens will insist that the City shall make arrangements with a view to their needs and convenience. Indeed the experience of Boston's street railways has shown that this alone is sufficient protection against unjust treatment.

We believe that a perpetual franchise is the worst possible form of franchise ; that a short fixed term franchise is only less objectionable in view of the rapid and complicated development of the local transit situation. That a short term franchise which can be retaken by the city on definate terms, relieving the concessionary of as much risk as possible is most to be desired.

Respectfully submitted,

CITY PLAN COMMITTEE, MUNICIPAL ART SOCIETY,

CALVIN TOMKINS,
Chairman.

Municipal Art Society
of
New York.

BULLETIN No. 20

COMMITTEE ON CITY PLAN:
CALVIN TOMKINS, Chairman.
JOHN DE WITT WARNER,   J. G. PHELPS STOKES.
FREDERICK S. LAMB,   CHARLES R. LAMB,
MILO ROY MALTBIE,   HENRY W. SACKETT.

JANUARY 12, 1905.

To the Honorable, The Rapid Transit Commission of The City of New York:

GENTLEMEN—In the construction of the first subway, your honorable body demonstrated the practicability of underground transit in New York. This constitutes a notable achievement, for which, however, the City has paid a high price in the terms of the seventy-five year Belmont contract. It should now reap the full benefit of its first experiment. Subway transit is no longer in the experimental stage and the City is in a position to bargain advantageously for its future transit facilities.

The plans recently proposed by your chief engineer have the merit of being definite, if not comprehensive in character.

In Manhattan they alternately provide for the convenience of the Interborough and the New York City Railway Companies, but do not meet the needs of the city.

In the Bronx they provide for three separate elevated extensions of the Interborough system and for a short spur, being the continuation of the proposed Lexington avenue line to One Hundred and Forty-ninth street, which is available for both companies.

In Brooklyn they provide for the extension of the Interborough system by way of the Eastern parkway and also via Fourth avenue, and for a possible new route by way of a proposed Governor's Island tunnel to the Battery.

In General.

With the exception of the last noted possibility, which as proposed is generally regarded unfavorably in Brooklyn, all of the lines are primarily laid out in the interest of existing corporations, and to this extent bear out the policy of your honorable board, so lucidly set forth by the Hon. Seth Low in his letter to your president, dated May 12, 1903. This policy presupposes the dependence of the city upon existing transportation corporations for additional facilities. If persisted in, we believe it will be found most injurious to the efficient development of the City's ultimate transit plan and the occasion for the alienation of the most important franchises for a small part of their value to the people.

The city is not dependent upon existing transit corporations. They are dependent absolutely upon it, and at the present time upon you. Underground transportation of passengers, gas and electricity in the interest of the community will be determined by the new subways and their control. With the exception of the subway now built, the City is in complete possession of all its possible underground highways. It should not forget or surrender this advantage. New subways should not be made dependent upon those existing or upon the private surface lines of the city, but should be planned with a view to their most effective and profitable operations by other corporations as well. Only by such open and general competition for licenses to operate can the best and cheapest bids and service be extracted from those best qualified to render them.

If you have any doubt that our citizens now wish that full and constant control of all facilities to be planned by you should be retained by the City, and private corporations excluded from any part therein—except such service as, from time to time, for periods always terminable at its option, the City may require—we urge that you procure a referendum on these points; and meanwhile refrain from in the least forestalling the situation.

Recalling the "Bostwick Bill," we cannot ignore that your intent may be as promptly as possible and for a long term of years, to put the control of New York's transit facilities into the hands of one or more of the private corporations, whose property is included in Mr. Parsons' scheme—thus indefinitely postponing City control, except after costly condemnation of franchises now donated. We do not question the sincerity of the conviction (if it is yours) that the public is too little fitted for greater control to be trusted therewith. But, as you appreciate, the property in question is that of our citizens—not your own. They have a right to speak for themselves, and should be given the opportunity to do so.

Moreover, we cannot assume you claim such omniscience that you can any better foresee what New York will need 25, or 50, or 75 years hence than did your distinguished predecessors in public service, who gave away our franchises, bungled our charter and straight-jacketed our city with its present block system, how seriously they were hampering the city they loved.

The plans proposed by Mr. Parsons are a particularly frank statement, in transit engineering terms, of a proposition to surrender the control of Rapid Transit throughout the greater city for generations to come. We respectfully urge that the City should never lose control of any of its franchises for any material period; and that no such plan should be seriously considered—at least until our voters shall have directly consented to such disposition of their own rights—not to say those of their descendants.

Specific Criticism.

We respectively note the following objections in detail to the routes as prepared by your chief engineer:

1st. They are more or less dependent on the Interborough and N. Y. City railway companies, and their construction will tend to make the City itself more dependent upon these corporations.

2d. They are crooked lines not adapted for modern express service which is the essential requirement of the Bronx and Harlem districts.

3d. Elevated lines in the Bronx and elsewhere are undesirable, and expensive as regards damages to abutting property owners.

4th. Lexington avenue is too narrow for efficient service at the present time.

5th. They do not adequately relieve the congested East Side tenement section.

6th. We object to deflecting the north and south bound tracks on Manhattan laterally through Twenty-fourth and Twenty-fifth streets, and particularly through Thirty-fourth street. Passengers and not trains should be transferred at right angles in Manhattan; danger and confusion will otherwise ensue. The mistake of conducting north and south travel through Forty-second street to the detriment of east and west travel on that street should not be repeated. Before the completion of the Pennsylvania Railway Station, Thirty-fourth street will be needed for a transverse road or moving sidewalk, and subsequently additional east and west streets in that vicinity will be urgently required for subways to relieve the growing congestion which is too evident already.

7th. The Eastern parkway route in Brooklyn is simply an extension of the Belmont System now building in that borough and extended to New York via the Joralemon street tunnel, which will probably be insufficient at its very inception for the travel already intended to pass through it.

8th. The Fourth avenue route via a proposed Governor's Island tunnel to the Battery does not meet Brooklyn requirements since it avoids, as at present planned, passing through the civic centre of that borough.

9th. The Fourth avenue route via Manhattan Bridge, reported on at your request, is deprecated by your chief engineer, although it is the only one of the Brooklyn routes proposed which can be operated independently of the existing Belmont system. We believe this route to be desirable if maintained under City control.

10th. No relief is provided for the congestion at the Brooklyn Bridge or for the growing disorder at the Williamsburgh Bridge. In view of the fact that your honorable body has already greatly complicated the situation at the former bridge by permitting the line and station of the Belmont subway to obstruct direct underground access to the bridge, we believe it is especially incumbent upon you to provide some means of alleviating the disgraceful daily melee at City Hall.

11th. The routes as proposed do not constitute a comprehensive plan. Such a plan we are aware must of necessity be sketchy and tentative, open to fair and interested criticism and subject to many subsequent changes. But a comprehensive plan which shall include the future possibilities of every north and south avenue on Manhattan.—Arterial transverse lines to Long Island and New Jersey by bridges and tunnels.—The intertransit relations of Queens, Brooklyn and The Bronx,—and finally, a Richmond tunnel by way of the Narrows or Bergen Point, or both, should not longer be delayed. Only by such planning in advance can inextricable confusion detrimental to the city's growth and welfare be avoided. You have also made this statement (see R. T. Com. Report, 1902).

The essential principle of continuous municipal control over all future routes we respectively submit has so far been avoided rather than recognized by your honorable body. After having established the entire practicability of subway transit at the expense of committing the City to the Belmont contract, you have recently issued a certificate for another franchise, not for a shorter term, but in perpetuity, to the New York and Jersey Company. In contradistinction to this policy we believe that all future licenses should provide, to use your own language: " That in case any municipal necessity shall arise, then upon the requirement of the board or the City the location under the streets of such passenger subway shall be changed or, if necessary, such subway entirely closed or surrendered." This, of course, should be joined to a provision for reasonable indemnity and notice to the concessionary. The City should, however, reserve the right under the above limitation to recover at any time, any grant of underground facilities. The basis for compensation may well be liberal, particularly in early years, and where private capital is involved, as is likely to be the case in increasing instances, now that the experimental risk has been eliminated. Only by such continuous City control, maintained through the power of recovery, can an adequate transit plan be evolved and adapted to the rapidly changing conditions incident to the phenomenal and complicated growth of the city.

A street franchise in perpetuity is a legal anomaly:

* * * "*there are no such things as vested rights*
"*which can interfere with the power of the community*
"*to do those things which are essential for its growth, its*
"*safety and its progress in civilization.* Improvident
" grants have been made; but, when they come in contact
" with the superior rights of the people, indemnity may be
" claimed and awarded, but their existence cannot be
" pleaded as a bar to improvement. This proposition is
" true not only of those companies which have their works
" under the streets, but of all companies which occupy them
" for any purpose whatever. The only theory upon which
" the rights of private corporations to use the public streets
" has ever been adjusted, is that they give greater facilities
" to the purpose for which the streets were created.

" But *the right of the City to require streets to be used*
"*in such manner as will, from time to time, promote the*
"*general convenience of the community is unquestion-*
"*able.*"

(Message, A. S. Hewitt to Board of Aldermen, 1888.)

It is consequently evident that the term of the grant only affords the basis for litigation as to indemnity in case the necessities of the City shall require its reacquisition. In other words, a perpetual or definite term grant under the complicated and rapidly changing conditions which exist, means that the City grants transit privileges for the present and largess in the future if its necessities shall require it to resume the grant. This is not right. While the concessionary should only be called to undertake the operating risk, which he does in any event,—the City should by reimbursing him on a valued basis for any part of the construction to which he contributes, be empowered to recover the grant by so doing.

It might be added that, in view of rapidly developing public sentiment, it is manifestly unwise and unsafe for officers of public service corporations to expose their stockholders to the risks incurred by a policy at variance with public interest and sentiment.

Alternative Suggestions.

On the map appended we indicate certain Manhattan, Bronx and Brooklyn routes in contradistinction to those presented by your chief engineer and which we venture to assume will better meet public convenience, particularly if kept under municipal control as above proposed.

As with those heretofore proposed the Manhattan routes now suggested are intended as examples only, illustrating the principles which we believe should be followed.

1st. A First Avenue Route—From Mount Vernon to the Battery, via Boston road, Third avenue, Willis avenue, First avenue, Allen street, Canal street, Bowery, Park row and William street, with extensions to Brooklyn and later to Richmond,—will provide a most efficient express service by a comparatively straight four-track road to lower Manhattan, with two-track continuation, relieving the east side congestion, and to an extent the congestion at the Brooklyn Bridge as well, by means of a station near the present bridge terminal and opening thereon, constituting in effect a back door to the bridge. Such a route will also tap each of the East river bridges, which will act as feeders to it. It is unquestionably the most profitable and desirable route which can be laid out at the present time, both for the City's interests and the interests of the prospective operating company. If properly marketed, the City should realize the most advantageous terms as regards transfers,* contributing capital, and right to retake; which constitute the three essential items in municipal bargains for any route. Direct contribution to the City's treasury being a matter of minor importance in connection with the initial contract for any road.

2d. The proposed "Fifth Avenue Line" forms a loop at the Battery with the First Avenue Line, by which it also connects with Brooklyn and Richmond. From the Battery it runs directly north through Greenwich street, West Broadway, Fifth avenue, Jerome avenue to Yonkers line. It is the best of the more important suggestions we have received since our former memorial (Bulletin 14) was put before you. Its advantages are three— It serves the most busy and crowded downtown district of central Manhattan, and the Harlem and Bronx sections, where present facilities are lacking or overcrowded.—By the directness of its route, it is an ideal central "express" line, and gives The Bronx rapid transit to its north boundary, better than the service upper Harlem now receives from the present tortuous subway.—Finally, it not merely connects closely with the Grand Central station and Pennsylvania subway, but makes accessible the parks, libraries, museums and gardens of Manhattan and The Bronx.

3d. A bridge subway loop, crossing the city and connecting the Williamsburg, Brooklyn and Manhattan bridges. Such a loop is submitted as an alternative for the separate bridge loops proposed recently by this committee in its Bulletin No. 14. It will be more convenient than the plan proposed by Bridge Commissioner Best and President Littleton, for connecting the bridges on the east side of the city by an elevated road through Centre street in that it will serve the convenient distribution of passengers as well as the requirements of the Brooklyn Rapid Transit Com-

---

*The question of transfers is inevitably to play an important part in any general system, and the best development of that system and of the city and its environs demands that the subject of transfers be considered in its whole scope, and in advance, and that the City should always retain power to require that they be given and accepted by the several subsidiary lines embraced in the general subway system, under equitable conditions.

(Extract, Merchants' Association Memorial to Rapid Transit Commission, December 15, 1904.)

pany for car shunting purposes. Furthermore, it will not disfigure the city.

4th. A bridge subway loop across Manhattan from the Blackwell's Island Bridge via Fifty-ninth street and Sixty-sixth (or Seventy-second) street. Provision for this should be made in advance of the completion of the bridge, as congestion there is already the cause of great local inconvenience.

5th. The avoidance of elevated railroad structures.

6th. An independent municipally controlled system of Brooklyn and Queens trunk subways, radiating from the terminals of the East river bridges, and extended in sequence of need into Brooklyn and Queens, beginning with the Fourth Avenue Line via Manhattan Bridge, which passes through the civic centre of Brooklyn and is urgently needed; and substituting for your proposed dependent Eastern parkway route one extending from the Manhattan Bridge via Fulton street, Gates avenue, Broadway–Fulton street to East New York. The extension of other Brooklyn and Queens lines are generally indicated in the map. We have also noted, but for later construction, and with the connection to the civic centre of Brooklyn, the Governor's Island tunnel proposed by Mr. Parsons, with its extension along Hamilton avenue, Prospect avenue and Ocean parkway to Coney Island. Over this trunk route to the Battery and up Fifth and other north and south Manhattan avenues, the City should maintain constant control, as it provides a most efficient through service and a most effective check upon the Belmont grants. Other suggestions for longitudinal and transverse lines on Manhattan and to New Jersey, together with a general statement of principles involved in New York rapid transit, are contained in Bulletin No. 14, recently issued by this Society, a copy of which we also beg to submit herewith.

Respectfully submitted,

CALVIN TOMKINS, Chairman.

JANUARY 12, 1905.

Oversized Foldout

Municipal Art Society
of
New York.

BULLETIN No. 24.

COMMITTEE ON CITY PLAN:

CALVIN TOMKINS, Chairman.
JOHN DE WITT WARNER,   J. G. PHELPS STOKES,
FREDERICK S. LAMB,   CHARLES R. LAMB,
MILO ROY MALTBIE.   HENRY W. SACKETT.

MAY 11, 1905.

To the Honorable Rapid Transit Commission of The City of New York:

GENTLEMEN—The report of your Committee on Plans and Contracts, dated April 13, 1903, says:

"The time seems now to have arrived in which an "attempt should be made to plan a system of Rapid Tran- "sit Railroads at least partially commensurate with all the "needs of the present city."

With a notable exception, the proposed lines which your committee indicate in the above noted report seem to us to be both comprehensive in character and, generally speaking, well adapted to the present and future needs of the city, following as they do well-defined lines of travel to and from lower Manhattan.

It is to be borne in mind, however, that the north and south avenues of Manhattan and the approaches to Brooklyn via Broadway, Fulton street and Flatbush avenue in that borough constitute the keys to the entire rapid transit situation of the city. These transit lines your committee now proposes to utilize, and, in doing so, we would respectfully

urge upon your attention the paramount importance of so contracting for their use that the City shall maintain control over them sufficient both for the subsequent extension of its rapid transit system and for maintaining cheap and efficient service, including a system of free transfers. To illustrate:

It is now proposed to extend the north and south lines of Manhattan for short distances only into The Bronx. Adequate provision on a single fare basis should now also be made for further northerly extensions of these routes within a reasonable time. Again, power should be reserved to the City to extend the much needed crosstown lines proposed by your committee, in the near future, to Long Island and subsequently to New Jersey, and also to enforce free transfers at intersecting points with north and south Manhattan lines. The Interborough System has agreed to this last principle, and by so doing has in a sense established the minimum market price for subway concessions between the boroughs. Such a system of transfers once established between new lines will soon of necessity compel a like general observance by existing transit companies.

There will not be found in Manhattan sufficient opportunity for north and south subways into which can be conducted trains coming from Long Island and New Jersey. Rather, what is needed by east and west bound passengers crossing Manhattan is, not a continuous ride through any *one* north and south avenue in that borough, but the opportunity to transfer to *all* such avenues at intersecting points. It is now in your power to obtain this essential factor for the lateral development of the city. Without it the Long Island and New Jersey sections of the Metropolitan District will be placed at a permanent disadvantage, and the development of the city as a whole will be retarded. In this connection we would quote from a recent report of the Merchants' Association, as follows:

" The question of transfers is inevitably to play an
" important part in any general system, and the best devel-
" opment of that system and of the city and its environs

"demands that the subject of transfers be considered in
"its whole scope and in advance, and that the City should
"always retain power to require that they be given and
"accepted by the several subsidiary lines embraced in the
"general subway system, under equitable conditions."

We believe that in no effective way can sufficient municipal control be maintained over transit corporations to accomplish the above results except by a system of short-term leases, coupled with the power of the City to recover the grants, if needed, on payment of stated indemnity. Your Honorable Board has made effective this principle in connection with the Dey street grant to the Hudson and Manhattan Company, the clause in that grant reading as follows:

"In case any municipal necessity shall arise, then, upon
"the requirement of the board or the city, the location
"under the streets of such passenger subway shall be
"changed, or, if necessary, such subway entirely closed
"or surrendered."

It may be noted in this connection that the operating contract between the Brooklyn Rapid Transit Company and the City, for the use of the Brooklyn Bridge, may be abrogated by either party on three months' notice; also that the electrical conduits in the city may at any time be repurchased by the City at a valuation 10 per cent. in advance of their cost.

The probable utilization of private capital in large part, for the construction of new subways makes it all the more imperative that a sufficient degree of control shall be maintained. The Interborough Subway (paid for by the City) is declared by the Rapid Transit Act to be a part of the highways of the city. Privately built roads, however, are not so described by the act, and for that reason their uses should be the more carefully guarded.

The evident desire of the New York, New Haven and Hartford and the Pennsylvania steam roads to avail themselves of the subway system of the city, marks a distinct and interesting transition in the use of the city's subways. As a result of the local electrification of these roads, and of the New York Central from Croton south, it is evident that the distribution and collection of their passengers can be most advantageously effected by running the coaches of these steam roads through the subways. Provision for this should now be made as regards height and width of the tubes, curves, grades, etc.; at the same time the necessity for a larger degree of municipal control, to prevent the local city transit system from being disadvantageously made subservient to the powerful interests of the steam roads of the country at large, becomes most obvious.

We heartily commend your discrimination against elevated railroads, and trust the Borough of The Bronx may not be handicapped by the future imposition of such roads to its comparative disadvantage with the rest of the city.

We desire to take exception to your proposal to deflect north and south bound traffic in Manhattan through 25th street, 34th street, 35th street and 36th street.

The street system of Manhattan above 14th street, excepting only the line of Broadway, is exceedingly simple, consisting of straight lines running north and south and east and west. Obviously, the lines of underground travel north and south should follow the north and south street lines; and the lines of underground travel east and west should follow the east and west street lines. Speed in transit, and the convenience of residence and business alike, make this so apparent that the defective 42d street turn in the existing Interborough Subway need only be referred to to condemn the proposal. The convenience of the existing local and steam road companies should in this matter be made subservient to the more important interests of the people of the city. **A crosstown line through 34th street, from river to river, should be made to serve all these interests by contract provision for free transfers at all north and south intersections, and provision should also be made as indicated for later extension of this subway to Long Island and New Jersey.**

The deflection of north and south subways through 34th street between Third and Eighth avenues, and a like deflection of the

Interborough road through the line now constructed in 42d street, in connection with the presence of the two great steam road stations on and near these streets, can only result in great future congestion and confusion. While it may be, and probably is desirable, that the trains of the steam roads should have access to the city's subways, the local travel should not be made to suffer as a consequence. The deep-level tracks of the Pennsylvania subways through 32d and 33d streets might more properly be connected with the tracks of the New York, New Haven and Hartford Railroad and those of the New York Central systems at 42d street, through a similar deep connecting subway constructed for the transfer of their own trains. Such a subway would not necessarily interfere with the local transit system of the city.

The diagonal line of Broadway intersects both Fifth and Sixth avenues. Any plan for the utilization of this principal thoroughfare should also include and clearly set forth its relation to the future subway uses of these two avenues. It is now apparent that all of the north and south streets of Manhattan will be required to their utmost capacity for future subways, and their future availability to this end should be preserved.

The loop via Fulton street, Flatbush avenue, Eastern Parkway and Broadway, together with the cut-offs through Lafayette, Gates and Bedford avenues, command the entire Brooklyn transit situation, and should always be maintained under City control.

President Orr's statement, as reported in the press:

"That the lines of transit in Manhattan must be in "favor of uptown routes, and all crosstown routes must "run beneath the uptown routes"—

we believe is sound and encouraging. This principle once firmly established will prevent much confusion and expensive rearrangement in the future.

The recent action of the Legislature will now enable your Commission to provide pipe galleries in connection with new subways, to the great advantage of the City as regards maintaining the surface of its streets, and also to properly control the public service corporations supplying gas and electricity.

Arcaded subways should be provided under congested streets, such as lower Third avenue, 14th street, 23d street, 34th street and 59th street; the convenience of entrance to the trains will thus be facilitated and abutting property enhanced in value by the additional street frontage obtained. An interesting example of this construction is to be noted at the subway station adjacent to the 23d street entrance of the Interborough system.

All franchises should expire concurrently with those recently granted. The date of the expiration of the McAdoo franchise through Ninth street and Sixth avenue might very properly serve as the index for all.

The Interborough franchise is incomplete at present, especially as regards its extension to the north, and we believe that the interests of the city will be served by granting to this company, on terms favorable to the City, a northerly extension through Lexington avenue, with provision for later extension south in a straight line as well.

To summarize, we respectfully submit that the entire subway system should remain under City control; that north and south subways in Manhattan should be built as nearly as possible in straight lines from the Battery north, and that east and west subways in the same borough should be conducted through the principal lateral streets, from river to river, with a view to their ultimate extension to Long Island and New Jersey,—and that a free transfer system between these two classes of subways, at intersecting points, should be provided for the future.

On behalf of the City Plan Committee of the Municipal Art Society, I remain,

Respectfully,
CALVIN TOMKINS,
Chairman.

NOTE.—The following Report has been approved by the Executive Committee of the New York Board of Trade and Transportation, at a meeting held this day, August 31, 1905, and will be submitted for the consideration of the Board at its meeting, to be held in the rooms of the Board, Wednesday, September 27, 1905, at 12.15 o'clock P. M.

FRANK S. GARDNER,
Secretary.

The rapid growth and development of the metropolitan district of New York, including Westchester County, Long Island, and the four northern counties of New Jersey, will make this City the greatest city of the world. Its harbor facilities and its unrivalled accessibility of approach from the West through the Hudson and Mohawk valleys are of more than national significance, since the City is so situated as to make it the centre of exchange. for those countries situated between the Rocky and Ural Mountains, whose commerce is tributary to the North Atlantic basin. The rail and water bound commerce of the world coming to it is the cause of the present greatness of the City and will control its future destiny as well. If the City is to take full advantage of its natural opportunities it must balance outside transportation to and from its gates by an adequate system of internal transport, both for passengers and commodities. Unless such a system of cheap and rapid transit shall be provided its growth and efficiency will be seriously retarded.

Commercial needs and social opportunity outweigh all other considerations. Increase of population without consequent increase of congestion constitutes the crucial City problem. Distribution of population over an ever widening area is the best solution and adequate and cheap transport between home and work the first need to this end. Since the opening of the Erie Canal no event of equal importance to the City has transpired until the present subway was built. In the construction of this first subway the Rapid Transit Commission has demonstrated the entire practicability of underground and under harbor transit. This constitutes a notable achievement, for which, however, the City has paid a high price in the terms of the seventy-five year Belmont contract. It should now reap the full benefit of its first experiment. Subway transit is no longer in an experimental stage, and the City is in a peculiarly advantageous position to bargain for its future rapid transit facilities.

The prompt development of its subways by the City through the agency of the Rapid Transit Commission on a grand scale is now imminent—the immense and unprecedented powers entrusted to the Commission, together with certain equally unwise legislative restraints placed on its power to contract for the City's interest—the fact that the franchises now under consideration by it include the control of the most important trunk line routes leading to the business centre of the City, the untrammeled possession of which by private corporations may seriously prejudice the subsequent development of a comprehensive plan of City transit—constitute sound reasons for a careful public scrutiny of the whole question of City transit at this particular time.

Lower Manhattan constitutes both the objective and departing point for the daily tides of travel. The strain on facilities incident to the rush hours in the morning and in the evening; the long, narrow configuration of the island, with its crowded and insufficient transit lines converging at the south; the tidal water belt which surrounds it on the east, west and south; its tall buildings, housing an unprecedented factory, office and tenement population; its street system planned in many respects for obsolete conditions—all these add difficulties to our transit problem.

It is evident that the greatest degree of congestion is now and will continue to be localized in lower Manhattan, and that this congestion tends seriously to increase in direct proportion to the growth of the whole city, and as transport facilities to and from other boroughs are made more adequate. These conditions offer additional reasons why the situation should be promptly and broadly dealt with before the opportunity shall have been forestalled.

For many years it has been the custom to farm out the privilege of passenger transportation within the City of New York to numerous traction companies for long terms and without adequate guarantee for controlling or extending service. Exploitation of these privileges for dividends and stock-watering profits has resulted in a congested and unsatisfactory service, which is being only temporarily relieved by the present subway.

So far as concerns the public, the great transport interests of New York constitute a single combine of three mutually jealous groups, the controlling interests steadily trending more perfectly to coalesce, i. e., Interborough, controlling the Manhattan and Bronx elevated and subway systems, the Brooklyn subways and the Queens surface railway lines; the New York City Railway Company, controlling the Manhattan and Bronx surface lines; and the Brooklyn Rapid Transit, controlling the elevated and surface lines of Brooklyn. In addition there is to be considered the local influence of the New York Central Railroad, which company is engaged in great terminal improvements and is preparing to install electric traction south of Croton; and the local influence which the Pennsylvania Railway Company will exercise through the agency of its tunnel, its Brooklyn and Bronx Belt line, and the community of interests which exists between it, the New York, New Haven & Hartford Railroad and New Jersey and Long Island steam and trolley lines.

In extending its own system of underground roads the City may well be served by utilizing, through short term leases, the experience acquired by the management of these corporations. But no such steps should be taken as shall place the essential features of the municipality owned system beyond the power of the City to control them.

The custom of farming out transit privileges for long terms to private corporations has proved its complete failure in practice. Contractual obligations for service and improvements, however stringently drawn, have been uniformly disregarded by the concessionaires. In the nature of things such obligations will continue to be so disregarded since private transportation corporations are necessarily organized and conducted for the distribution of dividends and the increment of ▬▬ stock values. Such corporations cannot of their own initiative keep pace with the evolution of public requirements, and have conclusively demonstrated their ability to avoid so doing.

Two other methods of municipal control are being availed of by American and European cities: 1st. Direct operation by the Municipality. 2d. Short term revocable grants.

We believe that whatever may be the policy of the City with reference to its other public utilities, that it will be premature for the City to attempt the direct operation of its railroad transportation at the present time, except under stress of such antagonism on the part of existing transportation corporations as is not likely to arise if the City shall maintain constant adequate control over them.

In contradistinction to the policy of long term grants we recommend that no grant shall be made for a longer period than twenty-five years, and that in the interim "in case any municipal necessity shall arise, then upon the requirement of the Board or the City the location under the streets of such passenger subway shall be changed, or, if necessary such subway entirely closed or surrendered."* At the expiration of the franchise if the City shall elect to take it back then the City shall pay to the concessionaire the appraised value of the physical plant at that time provided such plant was originally constructed at the expense of the concessionaire, but shall not include in such payment any part of the value of the franchise. If before the

---

*Clause inserted in contract between the City and the Hudson & Manhattan Co. by the Rapid Transit Commission, having reference to Dey St. subway.

expiration of the franchise it shall become expedient for the City to resume such franchise then the City shall have the right to do so by paying to the concessionaire the appraised value of the physical plant, at the time, if constructed at the expense of the concessionaire, and in addition, the appraised value of the franchise at the time of the recovery not exceeding   per cent. of the cost of the material structure exclusive of equipment. Such a procedure minimizes the risk taken by the City, and by the concessionaire, and consequently will tend to stimulate a prompt development of transit facilities. The concessionaire should only be called upon to undertake the operating risk—which he does in any event—and the City should by reimbursing him be empowered to recover the grant. The basis for compensation may well be liberal, particularly in early years, and where private capital is involved, as is likely to be the case in increasing instances, now that the experimental risk has been eliminated. Only by such continuous City control, maintained through the power of recovery, can an adequate transit plan be evolved and adapted to the rapidly changing conditions incident to the phenomenal and complicated growth of the City. The City is already committed to municipal ownership of its franchise, so that the proposed change is one of degree only.

The surface of the City has been exploited in private interest; underground New York, however, is still a virgin plain, not even bounded by the rivers, and under practically complete municipal control. If the interests of the City are not betrayed by its trustees it will continue to hold this position of vantage which it now occupies in bargaining for new facilities and for the improvement of old ones. If, however, new franchises are granted as mere extensions of existing franchises and are given without considering their relation to the entire question of transportation and its control, the City will soon lose the unique power of control which it now enjoys. In Chicago and Philadelphia the problem is to get back utilities which have been alienated—in New York it is simpler, consisting only in keeping what the City now holds possession of.

Short term revocable grants will tend to avert overcapitalization, with its consequent opportunities for exploitation and stock jobbery—and with its attendant risks both for the citizen and for the permanent *bona fide* investor in public service securities.

That precedents, in whole or in part, already exist in New York City for the further extension of this principle, is evidenced by the following ~~~~~~~ grants made by the City:

1. To the Brooklyn Rapid Transit Company for the passage of its cars over the Brooklyn Bridge, which privilege may be terminated by either party on three months' notice.

2. To the Hudson & Manhattan Company for a passageway through Dey Street, terminable "in case any municipal exigency shall arise."

3. To the New York and New Jersey Railroad Co. for a subway in Sixth Avenue and Eighth Street, terminable on payment of cost by the City at the expiration of a twenty-five year grant.

As far as practicable franchise grants should be made to terminate coincidently, this is especially true as regards trunk line franchises and their subsidiary branches. The failure to make this provision has caused great confusion in western cities and elsewhere where the twenty-year term prevails. In this connection we suggest that for the next five years the terms of city grants be made to terminate coincidently with the Sixth Avenue and Eight Street subway grant to the New Jersey & New York Railway Company.

The City should forever reserve the fullest control over its bridges and tunnels.

To all intents and purposes and as a consequence of its bridges and tunnels, New York will ultimately become a square or round city like Chicago or Paris, with the added advantages of cheap ▓▓▓▓▓▓ water transportation for commodities. The bridges and tunnels are, consequently, the keys to the successful development of passenger transportation in the interest of the passenger. Control over them will be eagerly sought by existing transportation companies, whose lines now constitute separate links of a temporary system which, for economy and convenience, must soon be welded together. The bridges and river tunnels in New York hold a position analogous to that of the municipal subway in the congested business district of Boston, the control of which by that city will enable it to regulate the entire elevated and surface systems which must perforce use the subway. The existing operating license over the Brooklyn Bridge previously referred to affords an admirable example of a working agreement between the City and its public service corporations, *in contra distinction to long term franchise grants*

" The question of transfers is inevitably to play an important part in any general transit system, and the best development of that system and of the city and its environs demands that the subject of transfers be considered in its whole scope, and in advance, and that the City should always retain power to require that they be given and accepted by the several subsidiary lines embraced in the general subway system, under equitable conditions." *

While it may be, and probably is, desirable that the cars of the steam roads leading to New York City should have access to the City subways, the local travel should not be prejudiced as a consequence. The evident desire of the New York, New Haven and Hartford and the Pennsylvania steam roads to avail themselves of the subway system of the City, marks a distinct and interesting transition in the use of the City's subways. As a result of the local electrification of these roads, and of the New York Central from Croton south, it is becoming evident

---
* (Merchants' Association Memorial to Rapid Transit Commission, December, 1904.)

that the distribution and collection of their passengers can in all probability be most advantageously effected by running their coaches through the subways. Provision for this should now be made as regards height and width of the tubes, curves, grades, etc.; at the same time the necessity for a larger degree of municipal control, to prevent the local city transit system from being disadvantageously made subservient to the powerful interests of the steam roads of the country at large, becomes most obvious.

We shall recommend that the Rapid Transit Act be promptly amended so as to grant the following additional powers to the Rapid Transit Commission, in order that the Commission may not be hampered in awarding franchises to the City's detriment:

1st. That the Commission be empowered to separate construction from operating contracts and so enabled to build cheaper, and contract for operation in a wider competitive field.

2nd. That unequivocal power be granted for the construction of pipe galleries in order that streets and pavements may be preserved from continual, expensive, and inconvenient disturbance; and also to facilitate adequate control over corporations supplying gas and electricity.

3rd. That the mandatory provision prohibiting a transit grant for a period less than thirty-five years be rescinded.

4th. That the City Charter and the Rapid Transit Act be so amended as to permit of municipal operation at any time. Section 73 now provides that the City may operate its franchise at their expiration. Bargains with private operators cannot, however, be advantageously made in the public interest unless the option to operate *at any time* shall be reserved to the City. The power to operate does not necessarily imply operation by the City, but rather that the City shall be placed in a position to obtain service to its best advantage.

We are convinced that the most potent corrupting force in Municipal government is to be found in the great private profit and the lax public control which are now characteristic of long term franchise grants, involving governmental functions which the City should not be divested of.

"The fundamental mistake has consisted in treating franchise grants as contracts, unalterable without the consent of both parties, like ordinary contracts concerning property. Governments, like individuals, may properly enough enter into contracts relating to property, and such contracts when made should be respected; but governments ought not by contract to divest themselves of governmental functions, as they do to an extent when they surrender partial control of the public streets, by giving to private interests definite term structural rights therein. The City can control completely only when it is in a position to terminate at any time the right of use claimed by any person or corporation that may choose to defy the will of the City in any respect. In other words, the grant terminable at the will of the governing authorities is the only kind under which the City can be sure of its ability to dominate the situation at all times."

Quotes from GEO. G. SIKES.
Atlantic Monthly,
March 1903.

RESOLUTIONS TO BE SUBMITTED WITH THE ABOVE REPORT.

Resolved, That passenger transportation franchises should not be granted by the City for terms longer than twenty-five years.

THAT at the expiration of grants the City shall have the option of recovering them on payment to the concessionaire of the appraised value of the physical plant at that time exclusive of franchise value, provided such plant was originally constructed at the expense of the concessionaire.

THAT the City shall also have the option of resumption at any intermediate period on payment to the concessionaire of the appraised physical value of the plant, if constructed at the expense of the concessionaire, and in addition the appraised value of the franchise at the time of resumption not exceeding   per cent. of the cost of the material structure, exclusive of equipment.

Resolved, That contracts for the use of any of the East River bridges by public service corporations be made to conform as nearly as practicable to the existing Brooklyn bridge contract between the City and the Brooklyn Rapid Transit Company.

THAT power be reserved to the City to exact transfers, under equitable conditions, over all municipally owned lines.

THAT franchises granted along general trunk lines of communication, be made to terminate coincidently with franchises for the subsidiary lines of each such system, and that during the next five years franchises be made to terminate on or before the expiration of the Sixth avenue and Eighth street grant to the New York and New Jersey Company.

THAT while it may be and probably is desirable that the trains of the steam roads leading to New York City should have access to the City subways—the local subway travel should not be prejudiced as a consequence.

THAT adequate provision on a single fare basis should be made now for the extension northerly of the projected Bronx lines.

THAT north and south subways in Manhattan should be built near the surface and as nearly as possible in straight lines from the Battery north, and that east and west subways in the same borough should be conducted on the next lower level through the principal lateral streets, from river to river, with a view to their ultimate extension to Long Island and New Jersey—and that a free transfer system between these two classes of subways, at intersecting points, should be provided for the future.

Resolved, That the Rapid Transit Commission and his Honor the Mayor, be requested, immediately upon the convening of the Legislature and before the City shall grant additional transit franchises, to demand that the Legislature so amend the Rapid Transit law as to give the Rapid Transit Commission the following additional powers:

1st. To separate contracts for construction from operating contracts.

2nd. To provide for pipe galleries.

3rd. To contract for operating periods of less than thirty-five years.

4th. To enable the City to avail itself, if need be, of the power of municipal operation.

ENGIN. - TRANS. LIBRARY
312 UNDERGRADUATE LIBRARY
764-7494
OVERDUE FINE - 25¢ PER DAY

DATE DUE